SOMETHING THAT MATTERS

Something that Matters

LIFE, LOVE, AND UNEXPECTED ADVENTURES
IN THE MIDDLE OF THE JOURNEY

A New Anthology from
The Wednesday Writers
of Oakland, California

Edited by
Elizabeth Fishel & Terri Hinte

with an introduction by
Elizabeth Fishel

Harwood Press
Oakland, California

Harwood Press
6134 Harwood Avenue
Oakland, CA 94118

Cover art and design: Linda Kalin
Book design: Phil Carroll and Linda Kalin

Printed in U.S.A.

First printing: June 2007

LIBRARY OF CONGRESS CATALOGING-IN-PUBLICATION DATA

Wednesday Writers.
Something that matters: life, love, and unexpected adventures in the middle of the journey/Wednesday Writers—1st. ed.
p. cm

ISBN-13   978-0-9728110-1-9
ISBN-10   0-9728110-1-x
1.Title. 2. Writing. 3. Memoir. 4. Anthologies.

Library of Congress Control Number: 2007926165

In memory of
Marian Magid

CONTENTS

OUR CHILDREN MOVE THROUGH US

PLEASURES AND PASTIMES

TRAVELS

THE WRITING LIFE

HEALING WORDS

INTRODUCTION

Elizabeth Fishel

FIFTEEN YEARS AGO when the Wednesday Writers first gathered in my Oakland, California living room, we wrote for our own private pleasure. From ten to twelve every Wednesday morning, fueled by strong coffee and soothed by lemongrass tea, we sank into soft sofas and sturdy rockers and wrote to ferret out what we knew. Then we strung the glassy beads of our separate truths into jeweled strands of overlapping stories. Part writing class, part support group, part literary salon, we became a writers' community that midwifed first-person essays about every stage around the life cycle. From the cozy safety of our weekly circle burst fervent stories of lives in transition when relationships redefined, families regrouped, jobs shifted, and moves, both inner and outer, scattered us into second acts.

Then four years ago our first anthology catapulted us from privacy into fifteen minutes of unexpected fame.

This is how it happened.

For several years the shadow of breast cancer had darkened our intimate circle, mirroring the national epidemic. Mothers, sisters, friends, and a sobering handful of the Wednesday Writers coped with it, wrote about it, and did their best to carry on. During the decade-plus we'd been meeting, twice the group attended memorial services for our writers whose lives had been cut short by cancer.

When my own mother also died after a valiant struggle with breast cancer, I needed to respond the best way I knew: with words. I wanted to do something that might make a difference in the lives of other breast cancer patients and raise money and awareness to battle this devastating disease that takes too many precious lives.

The Wednesday Writers mobilized with me in a two-step fund-raising plan. We hosted a literary event at the University of California San Francisco, "Healing Words," and brought together breast cancer survivors with acclaimed writers, headlined by Dr. Rachel Naomi Remen whose bestselling *Kitchen Table Wisdom* had inspired our own stories.

The event also turned out to be a publication party for our first anthology, *Wednesday Writers: Ten Years of Writing Women's Lives*, a heartfelt collection of first-person writing on the pleasures, pitfalls, and surprises of everyday life.

All of our contributing writers—30 for *Wednesday Writers* and 42 this time for *Something That Matters*—agreed to donate our entire proceeds to Bay Area breast care centers. Our first beneficiary was the Carol Franc Buck Breast Care Center at the University of California San Francisco, and our second anthology will benefit the brand-new, state-of-the-art Carol Ann Read Breast Health Center at the Alta Bates/Summit Hospital in Oakland, California.

Our collective spirit—multiple writers rallying multiple networks—has energized our project from the get-go. The combination of passionate personal writing by a group of ordinary women, many never before published, and the book's fund-raising goal touched a nerve in the San Francisco Bay Area with ripples nationwide. Terrific media attention greeted our first book, including a feature in *The San Francisco Chronicle* and many other publications. Spring, summer, fall, we were booked with readings and events and attracted such a following that we added another group we dubbed the Friday Writers.

And I was thrilled, as we all were, when our efforts paid off well—for two weeks running, a month after publication, *Wednesday Writers* hit the *San Francisco Chronicle*'s Bay Area paperback bestseller list, galloping right behind *Seabiscuit*.

As our group became higher profile, many of our writers grew more prolific and public as well. My coffee table overflowed with our members' writing published around the Bay Area and beyond. "40 articles published by 40!" vowed one of our writers who joined our circle in her late thirties; her fanny-on-chair perseverance, polished voice, and the group's faith helped her reach her goal by her 40th birthday. Suddenly we were all going to readings for Wednesday and Friday writers who were publishing their own books and contributing to other anthologies.

Three years and three printings later, *Wednesday Writers* has created a substantial gift to benefit breast health care in the Bay Area. We joke that like the British "Calendar Girls" we're women of a certain age who've raised money and attention for our cause. And we did it without even shedding our clothes.

The Wednesday Writers are mostly at life's midpoint now, still weaving youthful memories and dreams into stories, yet also imagining the path ahead with our words. Every decade provides more fodder, more cause for reflection. At midlife we strive more than ever to be the people on whom nothing is lost, as Henry James famously portrayed the writer's purpose. Our ordinary moments become exceptional in the retelling—a backyard barbecue on fall's first evening, a teenage son's cross-country meet, a father's wordless birthday appearance, a group of schoolchildren magpie-chattering in Monet's garden.

Our essays help us redesign the balance of our lives. We scribble our plans out for size in our group journal, make pleasures sweeter by recalling them, help each other find the right words to repair what's broken and move on. Our writing is the way we reorder what's most important, transform relationships, refashion work lives to release more time and space for new pursuits. Separately and together, we strive, in the poet Audre Lorde's words, "to touch something that matters."

Our territory is the moving target of the middle years, which our opening chapter, "Seasons of Our Lives," sets out to hold still. "autumn wind/ I pull another gray hair/ from my jacket sleeve," observes haiku poet Sue Antolin in "Artichoke Season." Heralding 40, celebrating 50, embracing 60, we counter whispers of mortality with writing's reinventions of self. Meanwhile, we grab "Tools of the Maintenance Trade," in Lori Rosenthal's phrase, to stave off time's damages.

In the chapter, "Our Parents, Ourselves," our mothers' and fathers' aging inspires a second look at the direction of our own lives. Watching parents grow frailer bonds us closer to them, prompting Mary Ford's reassessment in "Petite Madame" and Melanie Johnston's role-reversal in "Mothering Mother." It's now or never to put our passions at the center, as Christine Parsons's dreamer/father prods her in "Malt-o-Matic."

We explore the deepening intimacy of our liaisons in "Couples." If some marriages have ended sadly, as Swathi Desai's haunting "Loneliness" bares, others are given a second chance. Leah Fisher recounts her month-long time-out from a 25-year marriage in "Moving Out" and then her return home, feisty, unapologetic, but still pledged to her mate. Ronnie Caplane's column, "The Shoe," reports how unexpected widowhood side-lines her with grief, until she's spurred by a brief encounter into surprise resilience.

As "Our Children Move Through Us," our stories freeze-frame their growth spurts, the passages that require new roles and responses from us. Diana Divecha's "The Puja" documents her 13-year-old daughter's Hindu coming-of-age ceremony, celebrated by 16 bags of rose petals and blended relatives from Minnesota to Bombay. Risa Nye bakes and depicts one last "Enchanted Castle Cake" for her departing child, and Laura Shumaker stands aside so that her autistic son, now a teenager, can become "A Regular Guy." Cuddling fewer babies and more beloved grandbabies, we're proud to become 21st-century grandmothers, as Kathleen Faraday confides in her *Contra Costa Sun* column, "A Normal Grandma."

Meanwhile we declutter the corners of our lives and fill them with the "Pleasures and Pastimes" that matter most—family, friendship, music, cooking exotic meals and hand-me-down recipes, collecting, dog-walking, reading, day-dreaming, and discovering the distant corners of the world. "Travels" recounts journeys from Marienbad to Bahia, from painting in Giverny to making tiramisu in Tuscany, or globe-trotting with college friends turned "Traveling Grannies."

Above all we dedicate ourselves to "The Writing Life," knowing that "The Perfect Moment," as Kate Ruddle names it, may never quite come, but sandwiching time for writing into an already layered life. We are beyond excuses (in-laws arriving, children sick, dog-ate-my-homework) and have learned to just do it, jotting brainstorms on deposit slips, rough drafts between appointments, writing our dreams by flashlight in bedside journals.

We may fantasize about the month-long writing retreat to the mountain cabin. But these essays, simmered in the stewpot of daily life, record our reality now and will, we hope, inspire others to do the same.

Our work nourishes and renews us so we close with a chapter called "Healing Words" to reflect our shared dedication to the recuperative power of writing our way through uncertainty, illness, and loss. "After my cancer diagnosis I believe it was writing as much as medical treatment that enabled me to heal," explained one of the Wednesday writers, speaking for us all.

Two days before she died, our dear friend, admired community member, and fellow writer Marian Magid called to ask that I help find an audience for her last essay, "How to Help a Stubborn Sick Friend." "I'm on a mission," is how she phrased it. We are honored to include her essay here and dedicate this book to Marian's memory. Her call reminded me how much it matters to each of us that our words are read and heard. We write to touch each other's lives and to teach each other to treat the world more kindly. That was Marian's message and ours in *Something That Matters*. ∎

To order additional copies of *Something That Matters* or our first book, *Wednesday Writers: 10 Years of Writing Women's Lives* and for more information about the Wednesday and Friday Writers' groups, visit our web site, www.wednesdaywriters.com

WE GRATEFULLY ACKNOWLEDGE the support of the Alta Bates Summit Medical Center Foundation. The Carol Ann Read Breast Health Center is located in Oakland, California, at the Summit Campus of the Alta Bates Summit Medical Center. We are dedicated to providing compassionate, expert care that is easily accessible. Our mission is to offer the highest quality breast health and breast cancer care using state-of-the-art technology. For more information, please visit our web site: http://www.altabatessummit. org/clinical/breasthealth.html

SEASONS OF OUR LIVES

SPRING FORWARD, FALL BACK

Beatrice Motamedi

IT IS A THING we almost never do anymore: Just sit on the back-yard deck, and talk, and look up at the night sky.

Sirius is bright, and Cassiopeia has left her summer place and is whirling toward her winter home beneath the Little Dipper. My three-year-old nephew, Noé, points a stubby finger upwards and finds a bear. There is the familiar clink of bottle against glass as my father pours himself more wine. The night is velvet, black and soft as a fig. I lean back in my chair and for a moment I forget what time it is, what day it is, even what time of year.

It is fall, and it has taken us all season to experience this night of summer.

We should have had it in July, but we were too busy: Evan was in camp, Claire was taking classes, I was teaching, Andy was at work. We should have had it in August, but we were gone: Evan and Claire to their grandparents; Andy was in Cleveland, and I in Chicago. We could have had it in September, but there was school, and more work, and more traveling.

And so on to October. Only in California can you get a second chance at summer.

Going to the produce store this morning in search of fall vegetables, to my astonishment I found August in the aisles: sweet corn, white peaches, vine-ripened tomatoes, the heady perfume of fresh cilantro.

I bought it all, plus beef and salmon. Rushing home, I called my parents and my brother and his family and asked them to come over for dinner. We'll eat outside, I thought happily, on the deck under the big redwood tree just starting to drop its needles. I started chopping garlic, onions, herbs, swirling it all into a mari-nade with olive oil and sweet fig vinegar. I was in heaven.

Unfortunately, I was also in Daylight Savings time.

Which meant that as I chopped, minced, marinated, and stirred, the world was spinning and night was falling. Washing the rosemary, I glanced up through the window and saw that the sky had turned a suspicious shade of pearl, like the inside of an oyster. I looked at the clock, confused. *It's only 4 p.m. Where has the sun gone?*

By the time I realized my mistake, it was too late to change course. Andy went on setting the table outside. When my brother arrived, an hour later, the air was still warm but the light had fled, and the sky had gone from gray to plum.

Sensing impending disaster, the kids perked up. Evan went in search of the earthquake kit and his nightsticks. Claire found the candles. We scurried for flashlights, one for the table, one for the food, one to see the hand in front of my face as I grilled the beef.

By now it was 6 p.m. and we were stumbling in the dark like idiots. *Where are the chairs, what kind of batteries do we need, who sat on the tomatoes?* We poured more wine and made futile stabs at our darkened plates, hoping that our forks would come up with something edible. Noé pointed again at the sky and we exclaimed with delight. The stars, at least, were visible.

It's not often given to us to know the moment when the world shifts and life changes. The time you stop wiping the crumbs off your shirt and look up into the eyes of the man who will become your husband. The night when your child decides that this bedtime story will be the last. The instant when the cells in your breast, multiplying the way they always do, decide to speed things up a little.

Perhaps it's best we don't know when such moments happen; they might be too much for us to understand. But I do know when fall began, because I had that one last night of summer.

It was Sunday, October 10. And for a moment, everyone I loved was there.

ARTICHOKE SEASON

Susan Antolin

artichoke season
sharing my heart
I try
to slice it
evenly

Independence Day
I struggle to free myself
from a wet swimsuit

wet shiny red grapes
we swap stories
of summer

at the festival
in San Francisco
naked men and women
stare for a moment
at us

at the opera
replacing the lyrics
with my own failures

daughter sent to her room
I scrub old stains
on the kitchen counter

in a steady rain
the patio umbrella
with arms at its side
has no answers
either

the baby asleep
this morning's tea bag
floating in silence

one a.m.:
the palm of my hand
the curve of her cheek

tracing the line
of downy hair
behind my daughter's neck
will a lover
do this?

our child between us
we reach for each other
with our toes

news from Mars—
my toddler's searching hand
under my shirt

off the bestseller list
now what?
breakfast? or back to bed?

tomato seedlings—
my young daughter
shows me her muscles

swirls of steam
rising from my cup
into a slice of sunlight—
I was once
so free

in new sandals
unpolished winter toes
first day of spring

watching a stranger
read my words—I strain
to read his face

hot summer day—
over cold cherries, my son asks
is *this* haiku?

on our way
to march for peace
the kids bickering

sipping a beer
I agree to pumpkin pie
before dinner—
and what
of it?

autumn wind
I pull another gray hair
from my jacket sleeve

still composing
the goodbye I never said
September sky

uncooked spaghetti
barely in my grasp
I am not the mother
I wanted
to be

balanced on the fence
an abandoned tangerine
and the setting sun

dreaming of escape
I add "get passports"
to my to do list

STILL LIFE WITH FLOWERS

Suzanne LaFetra

THE FIRE SPUTTERS as cold rain drizzles down the 90-year-old chimney, while I unpack a trunk full of grinning, glittery skeletons, bone-white skulls of sticky, pressed sugar, the decorations for Day of the Dead. I never know just how my altar will turn out. I select armloads of flowers, letting my mind and eyes wander to see where the color and texture and scent of the cut beauties leads me.

Every year my altar is different, and every year I wonder what it will hold in the future. I set out the pictures of the family ghosts and zip forward to an imagined future. Will my husband's freckled smile grace this table next year? Will I sprinkle fiery orange marigold petals across pictures of my parents? How many funerals will I attend between now and the future? A friend once told me that each year, we pass by what will be the anniversary of our death, unknowing. Day of the Dead reminds me. I cannot know, but I feel the sharp poke of the spur, reminding me that it will come.

When I began the tradition of building an altar for *El Dia de los Muertos*, I was 15 years younger, so young, unscarred by death. My altar that year held the collar of my dog, Coyoacan, who died from a snakebite. A few years later, my grandmother's photo joined the incense and marigolds. Over the years, my altar has held the keys to a failed business, a newspaper from September 11, a picture of my gray cat, who died on Christmas Day. Each year, my altar becomes more crowded, the flowers tucked around memories of what is no more.

The amaranth is wrapped in a cone of newspaper, and I tear it open, to see headlines of the war, two weeks old. I unwrap a large, drooping olive branch, a prayer for peace. For the soldiers, there are pussywillows, stalks of corn, spiny artichokes, and marigolds. For their mothers, baby's breath and olives, forgiveness and healing. The war is making my altar spikier, more dangerous.

9

I slice open the plastic cellophane of a dozen tiny black roses, Black Baccara, they're called, their fingernail-sized buds a deep blackish purple. These are for Julien, my friend Naomi's three-year-old son, who died of leukemia on a perfect spring morning. With red-handled clippers I shear away the thorns and leaves, and poke the skinny stems into a thin-necked vase. To this I add baby's breath, surrounding the roses in snowy white. I hate baby's breath but somehow, I felt the altar needed it this year, that I needed it this year, that maybe Naomi needed it this year. My stomach knots when I begin to imagine her pain. Julien's death is making my altar more ominous.

I put another piece of paper, folded, at the back of the altar. This tiny chart is what I used to determine my exact ovulation, so that we could time our sex for pregnancy. My husband had a vasectomy this year; there will be no more babies in my body. There will be only older children, then teenagers, then adults, then only silences between phone calls. I put four stems of pussy-willows in a copper vase, blue with age. Then I tuck in tuberose, so sweet-smelling it is almost unpleasant. My children growing up is making my altar complicated.

I set out a picture of Rob, who was my lover in college. He died last winter on a basketball court, his heart stopped just as he made a lay-up, one sneaker untied. I imagine him staring into the blue sky, feeling his life slip away. He was 40, the same age I am now. A creased obituary from my hometown newspaper sits next to a grinning sugar skull. Darien was our high school's majorette, and she died last month, her breasts filled with cancer. People my age die, I am realizing. People I know. I balance long, twisted willow branches in the corners of my altar, and one tips, then falls. Age is making my altar more precarious.

I pull peppery petals from the *cempasuchitl* flowers, making a fist-sized pile of orange. I shape this into a heart, and light another candle, setting it right in the middle. I sit back on my haunches, and let it flow into me. The ache of time passing, the pain of humanness and mortality, the bittersweet knowledge that we are all just muddling through, that there is no escaping our mortal coil. And squatting in front of my altar, I hear the carillon bells of the clock tower a few blocks away. The bells toll, and for a moment I am frozen, knowing that someday my image will be on our family altar, too. And I bury my face in my hands, crying for a moment at the pain of being alive, and the agony of knowing that it's all too short.

And then, I hear my kids splashing in the bathtub, hear my husband holler at them that the floor's getting soaked. And I uncover my face, and feel the deep pull in my breasts to be with them, to bound upstairs to the wet, joyful chaos that is my life.

I lift up the last bunch of flowers, shaggy sunflowers in a brown paper cone. I've never included this happy flower on my altar before, they seemed too zealous, like they're trying too hard. But I bought them today without knowing why, and now, I stick their impossibly long stems into a tall, wide vase, and balance them in the very center of the altar. They stand alert at the back, sunny reminders that I must not forget to notice the color and scent of the beauty around me, even though the flowers themselves are dying, even though this is a memorial to the dead, even though we cannot shake off the heavy cape of mortality we wear. I see those bobbing, smiling heads and remember that this is what we have, and it has to be enough.

And then I run upstairs and rub my children with yellow towels, their warm pink skin turning pinker, and each one tells me all the reasons they do not want to go to bed. All that they haven't yet done. All that they haven't explored. All that they haven't finished. All that they haven't even started. All that they ache for—more time. *Please, more time.*

"I know," I tell my daughter in her perfect, curving ear. "I know," I whisper to my son, when he asks for the flashlight.

TOOLS OF THE MAINTENANCE TRADE

Lori Rosenthal

IT'S NOT JUST BOY SCOUTS who need to be prepared. Since most possessions are built to fall apart over time, they last a lot longer if you tend to their natural maintenance. At least that's what my mother, the Depression baby, always told me. Mom was a consummate master at extending the natural life of her belongings, and by extension ours, too.

Her sewing kit, a colorful, tangled collection of this and that housed in a holiday cookie tin, was her faithful companion. Mom and her magical sewing kit saved countless shirts, socks, and pairs of blue jeans from an early demise. She used leather polish for her always-pristine shoes and purses, and silver polish for her fancy cutlery. Elmer's glue was a ready tool in her hands for the destruction caused by her three children, who were rather hard on the lamps, living room knickknacks, and other breakables. Upon close inspection, you might think those repaired crack lines on our entire household lamp collection were some sort of unifying design feature.

Duct tape was Dad's contribution to the longevity lessons. He'd never met a fraying object that he couldn't revive with a few yards of the stuff. He brought home rolls of it from his auto body shop, and we wound it faithfully around objects in need, foot by foot. Lawn furniture seats, tennis racquets with sticky grips, aging sleeping bags and tents all came under his spell. When Mom sold the house last year, after 26 years as our family's home base, many of these items, duct tape still firmly intact, were finally retired.

During my looks-obsessed teenage years, I remember fondly the two personal-hygiene maintenance items that were staples in my life. I never left home without either my Maybelline mascara, or the clear nail polish of no particular brand that was my mobile pantyhose repair kit. Every girl needs a few tools of the trade. I'm sure they contributed to my successful passage from adolescence to young adulthood and beyond.

Standing as I am now on the cusp of a "certain age," I find that my assemblage of personal-hygiene maintenance products has expanded far beyond mascara and clear nail polish. My daily home-based routine relies on an increasing collection of concoctions and medications, including the all-day moisturizer with SPF 30 that I apply to my face each morning, as well as the little glass pot of age-defying all-night nourishment cream that I wouldn't dream of entering dreamland without. There are the calcium pills that I ingest to preserve the above-average bone density that I am lucky to have. And, in an honored place above the kitchen sink, there is the ever-present bottle of Ibuprofen, into which I dip regularly to erase the random aches and pains that plague my well-exercised body.

I also have a team of neighborhood beauticians and specialists on hand to function as co-conspirators in my battle against age and gravity. One of them shared with me her thoughts on aging on the eve of my 40th birthday. "Think of yourself as a beloved used car," she advised. "You're entering that time of life where maintenance makes all the difference." As more gray hairs encroach on territory where they simply do not belong, my hairdresser increases her efforts to create the decidedly gray-free hair color that I favor. As wayward eyebrows come marching across my brow, the kind that look and feel like insect antennae, a facial technician is there to thin them out of the eyebrow ranks. And my friendly dermatologist is called into action for twice-annual checks of face and limbs that basked so ignorantly in the unprotected sun of youth. I am now paying the price, as he regularly cuts, freezes, or otherwise disposes of tiny little precancerous intruders. Out spot, out, I say.

My newest recruits in this growing infantry of personal-maintenance tools are of the oral persuasion. I now rely twice daily on my Sonicare toothbrush to clean my teeth and their unfortunate neighbor, my receding gumline. At the dentist's suggestion, under threat of a potential root canal, I've also added a fitted plastic mouth guard to the nightly routine. This device makes it impossible for me to grind my teeth while sleeping, and may help prevent my gumline from receding even further. I laugh at the image of my husband and me crawling into bed each night wearing our respective custom-fit mouth guards. It is plastic on plastic at the moment that we say goodnight. But I know he understands. As a former Boy Scout and product of frugal parents himself, he too learned early in life to be prepared.

COMING OF AGE AGAIN

Mary Ford

MY 50TH BIRTHDAY, like my long-ago birthing plan for my son, who's now 14, was nothing like what I had planned. For Dan's birth, there were supposed to be low lights, music, and candles. What we got, of course, were three days of chemical inducers in a clattery hospital culminating in a tired, rushed, but ultimately triumphant midnight cesarean. For 50, my checklist included being filled with wonder, insight, and epiphanies, preferably on a mountain or beach; doors opened, perfect gifts, knowing looks, considerations right and left. What happened, of course, was less than ceremonial.

Dan had his first-ever ten-page paper due that day, so the night before was long and—ahem—fervent. I still delude myself that he needs company and support during these academic ordeals, and he cooperates by asking me to literally hold his head up while he types at 12:45 a.m. Did I help create this scenario or just respond to it? When I wake at 7 a.m. on my birthday morning, I've had only five and a half hours of sleep. So after remaining vertical for the requisite birthday hug and kisses from my husband Rob, I head back to bed.

At 10:10 I wake with a start, realizing that my yoga class (life-line to serenity and muscle tone) starts in 20 minutes. Running down the hall, I spy a suspicious long lump in Dan's bed; he has slept in and needs a ride to school immediately. With unequivocal resolve, I de-bed him, make a sandwich and have him in the car in eight minutes. Checklist: Mothering and dictatorial skills honed—check.

After pushing Dan out of my moving car onto the school side-walk at 10:26, I am only five minutes late for class. My yoga mates serenade me with birthday greetings from the floor with left legs up in straps, faces beaming. Halfway into our 90 minutes, I success-fully execute *Vasisthasana*, which involves holding myself up side-ways from the floor with one hand and one foot on the ground, the other hand wavering high above me. My whole body is shaking, but, by God, I do it. Belying my actual age and condition—check.

I'd planned to go to the beach, but it is rainy-looking, so I go home, read e-mails, and shower. Heck, might as well make those calls that have to be made. Momentous accession to practicality—check.

I have to get away from the house for those darn epiphanies, so I pack up my notebook and boldly and resolutely go to the carwash, sell my used books, and idly shop at the clothing store next door. Finally I park myself at Saul's to sip tea and write, but I am fresh out of epiphanies. I've been having waves of ideas regarding midlife angst for two weeks, day and night without respite, but now, *nada*. I write about my day so far, about how it doesn't need to be perfect, that satisfactions lie in the small things, etc., etc.

Rob calls. He's at Dan's baseball game. People are due at the house for a birthday dinner in an hour. Can I pick up the takeout he's ordered? I cheerfully say yes, feeling saintly. That way he can go home and prep. What a generous person I am! My life is filled with goodness, and I can help, even on this special day! I have an expansive, philosophical conversation with James, the young Chinese waiter from L.A. with the shaved head. My favorite Peking Duck is tucked into the trunk, and I head home to walk into the loving gazes of my friends and family. I haven't needed fanfare; I have a lovely family, a beautiful garden, and a vibrant life! The rest is unnecessary. What is important is the love that I can give and take among my friends, family, and community. Epiphanies come when you don't expect them, not when you lie in wait.

I pull into the carport, and Rob's car is not there. OK. Probably a last-minute errand.

I puff upstairs with the cartons, and no one is there. The dining table is littered with newspapers, pens, wrappers, and cups. A note from my friend Susan says she came an hour ago and waited for us, but finally decided to go home—was there no dinner? Is everything all right? Susan, with heart problems, who struggled to get up our 21 stairs and can't do it again in the same day. John, Kathy, and her son Chase are due in ten minutes.

I drop the food and madly start clearing the table. I call Susan to commiserate and apologize, and while I'm talking to her, Rob walks in. While I magnanimously did his pickup errand for him, he had stayed at the baseball game.

"It doesn't take that long to set a table, you know," says he.

"Especially when I clean up everything else, huh?"

"Don't do anything! It's OK! I'll handle it!"

"You'll handle it as people arrive, right? How long have you known me? Twenty years? How many times have I been delighted to wait till the last minute to set up the house for company? How many times have we had this conversation?"

Somehow my expansive philosophical stance has escaped me. I am left with my ordinary male husband and my ordinary outrage at not being pampered to my specifications. I continue in this highly articulate, entirely justified vein for several minutes.

Susan decides that she'll come back, and Kathy and company come 15 minutes late, and we are nearly ready for them. I talk with them about the recent events in the day, embellishing on its latest turn. We notice Rob is gone. Where has he gone?

"Maybe he's gone back to the game," chuckles Susan.

I freeze, think of that possibility. "I'm not going there."

"Oh, I saw, girl. You already went there," John says, laughing.

"Yeah, but I decided not to stay."

Rob returns shortly with the dessert. We sit down to dinner, pray our thanks to The Higher Power with two-fingered peace signs touching by fingertip around the table, the latest Ford/Lewis innovation to demustify the ritual. The food is delicious, and we plow into it. The conversation is rowdy, the volume is raucous. Stories are told. Susan gets a taste of Kathy, John, and Chase (one of Dan's best friends), and vice versa. Worlds connect. I read aloud snippets from an article about Brazil taped to the fridge. John twinkles. Kathy speaks softly and lovingly; Chase, Dan, Rob, and John talk music, sports, funny stories. It is a din.

Kitty Kat crawls up on an exhausted Susan's lap, then up on to her chest for a serious neck-licking/nursing session. Susan settles back with her eyes closed as we hurtle on with shouted jokes, stories, toasts. She is getting to see the Dan who comes out only with family. I smile inside.

Hours later we adjourn so that the boys can do homework. I kiss Rob and thank him for my dinner. There is not much after-taste of our earlier tango for me; I said what I needed to say. Don't know what got through to him, given the delivery. I wonder about him but know he is chewing on it, and has been gracious to change gears and leave the rehash for later. I check my e-mails, and write some notes for this story.

Rob's mom and sister call, as do many friends. For some reason, no one in my original family calls or sends a card this birthday, but they are not Bad Guys, and I can mostly accept them now for who and where they are. Although it *is* inconvenient that they are not the people with the thoughts and feelings that I had in mind for them, they're generous in other ways. The bucket that holds the love and self-esteem doesn't have as big a hole as it used to have. Letting go of Daddy's and Mommy's attention—check. Well, OK, one in a series of checks. And oh, yeah, there are 50 people coming over to celebrate with me on Sunday.

That is my day. Transcendent in its ordinariness, magnified only because of my heightened expectations.

On this birthday I continue to wrestle with my sense of purpose and accomplishment. My obsessive makeup is such that for the first half of my life, I silently counted the letters in the words that I spoke and others spoke to me, and I did this almost continuously. It gave me something to fill my mind with order. It soothed me.

Busyness has always been a rag doll in my arms. Up until six years ago, I had several high-visibility psychologist jobs. Titles, projects, clients, students, supervisees, long hours. Then, I quit psychology for an indeterminate length of breathing deeply. I went through a painful withdrawal and deflation from the recognition and obsessions of my work, which had begun to take away more than it gave me, because of what I expected it to fill in my life. When it hadn't filled me up, I had just worked harder.

I still sing in performances 40 or so times a year, serve on boards, mother, keep house, paint occasionally, write sporadically—

when something bubbles up and won't go away, or there's someone else's deadline to mind (I'm working on that one). I often feel indolent, though others who love me point out that I'm one of the busiest people they know.

Today I am not without ambition, standards, and expectations, not by a long shot. But I am more elastic about the nature and value of outcomes, with a shorter lag-time in adapting to altered circumstances. More important, I (blessedly) remember more often that a large part of what transpires around me has far less to do with me than I tend to think.

My biggest, greatest, dumbest secret is that the love I can feel now trumps a lot of my needing to troll for order or recognition. I am living more and more in my own constellation of loyal, true lights that don't blink and disappear based on their or my state of mind. I seemed to have joined the human race. It is a plainer, less glossy place than the places I made up in my mind when I was younger. For so long, I lived in the tower of my busy mind more or less by myself, and it is much cozier here, surrounded by the people I love.

SHE LOVED THE SIXTIES

Mary-Jo Murphy

I BEGAN WRITING New Year's resolutions five years ago. My life was changing into something unrecognizable, and I hoped to gain perspective a year at a time. I longed for a sense of hopefulness. Posting my yearly resolutions reassured me, marked a personal beginning. My desire for inner growth and focusing toward the future gave me confidence to move toward the years ahead.

A humbling thing I now know about my resolutions is that often the same maddening self-reform appears several years in a row. *Living in the moment, letting the past be gone, being generous of spirit.* My lists have offered me not only perspective and a sense of optimism, but endless opportunities to obsess about my failures and feel guilty about my imperfections. At best I have avoided stagnation. My struggles with my personal demons are reworded, time and again. My list of needed improvements should have its own aisle at Home Depot.

I am careful about what I resolve. Winning the lottery is out of consideration. Resolutions must relate to things over which *I* have control. I can't resolve to write a bestseller, but I can commit to fingers on the keys at regular intervals. *Butt in the chair. Fingers on the keys.* Stare with horror at a blank computer screen *for an hour daily. Submit your writing for consideration.* These behaviors I can control.

I have found that simple resolutions with complex intentions can be life-altering. Stalled after the demise of my 20-year marriage, when all I had expected to be my future was gone, I resolved to *make new memories.* Faithfully I pushed myself. Sometimes my efforts were simple. One week at a sushi bar I tried sea urchin. Not exactly brave, but that slimy morsel fulfilled my commitment to *have a new experience every week.*

Coupled with a grander scheme, to *learn to live again,* I took on things as personally awkward as accepting invitations to ski, sail, attend a dinner party, go on a date. I had outgrown sea urchins.

Unsure what my new life would look like, I intended to begin again, to *create a future*. What would happen next would have bits and pieces of my old reality and likely surprises. As time passed I became eager for new challenges.

A few years ago my divorce lawyer presented one. *Make money*. After six months of searching, I secured a job, which was to take me significantly out of my comfort zone.

The work to which I returned had been interrupted by further education, years of raising children, assisting with a spouse's career, performing volunteer work, and creative endeavors. Within three weeks of being hired, I uprooted my life in the Bay Area and moved to Southern California. *To have new experiences* took on new meaning.

Long ago I had resolved to *learn a second language*. I imagined fulfilling this goal in an exotic place, drinking margaritas. Instead I found myself counseling both English- and Spanish-speaking patients on their diabetes regimens at a county hospital. I attended classes weekly and studied vocabulary and grammar. I next resolved to *speak Spanish*. This is quite a different challenge from *learning* and closely resembles stage fright. I was careful not to modify *speak* with *well*. Resolutions must relate to things over which I have control.

The unspoken admonishment of my resolutions is always there. *Don't get lazy. Don't stand still. Don't let the years go by unnoticed, uncelebrated.* Which brings me to this year's resolution.

For the first time I wish I could include *stand still; don't grow; stay as I am*. This year's resolution will be both transforming and terrifying. This year's resolution will appear only once. I can't get out of this with a trip to a sushi bar. This year I resolve to turn 60!

How did this end up on my list? I was preoccupied. I should resolve to *never again be preoccupied*. My fifties were taken up with my sons' high school and college years, male midlife crisis, and my own menopause. I sold, bought, and remodeled a few houses in between. Even receiving my AARP card didn't shake my denial. I know I should have seen this coming, prepared, had a plan.

I knew sometime, somewhere I was going to have to fill in that age blank with the big 6-0, but I have no skills for aging. My problem is that I remember when 25 seemed old. I need to *gain perspective*. I need help.

This year the first of the baby boomers will begin this journey. I, a February baby, born in 1946, am in the forefront. As a group we were disinclined to trust authority, to ask for advice. But I need guidance. Who else has successfully crossed this milestone? I read the celebrity birthdays in the newspaper. Dionne Warwick is 65. Do you know the way to prevent decay? Connie Francis is 67. Who's sorry now? Cher. She's my age, and so is Rod Stewart. Though I heard he just had a baby with his new young wife. Rod is no help. I long for a sense of hopefulness. It has occurred to me that my plan to gain perspective might need to include *find a mentor*. I wonder if Judi Dench is available. And then I remember.

"You tend to come to me after you have already decided something," my mother says again. She knows I keep my own counsel. I never asked her advice before. I never thought she had any to give. I seldom wanted her ear. Even now, when my mother offers her perspective on love and life, grandchildren, retirement, I tune out. In some ways I'm still a know-it-all teenager. This year all that changes.

This year my mother celebrates 92 years. She put this turning-60 stuff behind her long ago. When I phone her, I hear voices in the background.

"I'm listening to books on tape," she tells me. An avid reader, she has recently had to adjust to life with macular degeneration. She has her own apartment. People come and go, home health aides, physical therapists, meals-on-wheels. But she lives on her own.

"Do you know how I put on my eyebrows?" she asks. My mother never left her bedroom in the morning without her makeup.

"I have no idea."

"I made a stencil. I just have to be careful that I have the eyebrow pencil and not the lip liner."

Last night snow fell in Connecticut, and this afternoon she tells me she's off to a Women's Club luncheon. A greeting card she recently sent to my five-year-old step-grandson was returned to her. She has more grandchildren and great-grandchildren and even great-great-grandchildren than I can count, but she remembers Cole's birthday.

"Take it easy," I advise, worried about her back, her footing, her eyebrows.

"I've learned to pace myself," says the woman whose mantra has been *It's better to wear out than to rust out*. "I socialize one day, sleep the next."

I tell her I'm planning a trip to Paris for my birthday.

"With that lovely man? How nice." I have *learned to live again*. She approves.

"Mother, I can't believe I'm going to be 60," I venture.

What's it like? I think. Aging? How do I do this? How does it look from your perspective?

"Mary-Jo," she says. "I loved the sixties. The seventies were great. I was so proud to make it to 80 . . ." She hesitates. "But the nineties make me nervous!"

As this year draws to a close, I review my past New Year's Resolutions. I will begin my new list with a slightly reworded repetition.

Enjoy this time in your life. Sixty is no big deal. I add another . . .

Resolve to *listen to your mother*.

THE TREE

Irene Sardanis

I'VE LIVED THROUGH more than 60 Christmas Eves, but the one I remember best took place in my family's apartment in the Bronx on a cold night in 1943. I was ten. My older brother was away in the Navy, somewhere in the South Pacific. My father was long gone. My two older sisters were away with relatives, and the responsibility for caring for my mother had fallen to me.

It was freezing outside that night and our tenement, too, was cold. The apartment was dark, save for the lone lamp in the living room, where I sat by myself, waiting for something to happen. Everything was silent, except for a noise coming from the kitchen, where the refrigerator made a groaning sound as if it were about to expire. My mother was lying, as usual, in her bed, with the covers up to her chin, her body slathered with Vicks and Ben Gay. For most of my life, this is the way I've remembered her: not sick enough for a doctor, not well enough to be on her feet. My father had left her two years before, and a day never passed that she did not curse him, or remind me of all that he had done to make her life miserable.

I fidgeted in my chair. Perhaps a knock on the door from a neighbor would break the deafening silence.

"This is Christmas Eve," I said to myself, "and we don't even have a lousy Christmas tree."

I sighed loudly, hoping my mother would hear me and do something. Anything. She hadn't even tried to get up and cook or bake something, or bring some holiday spirit, some small cheer, into the gloom.

After what felt like hours of dull despair, I couldn't stand it any longer. I went into the dark bedroom where my mother lay "ach, aching," as usual, bemoaning her bitter fate. For as long as I remembered, she'd complained to anyone willing to listen about the hard life she had bringing me up without the support of a husband. Once again that night, she spoke of the countless sacrifices she made for me, how she almost died in childbirth with me, and how I should never forget it.

Now I understand my mother better. Her marriage had been ill-fated from the beginning—arranged, sight unseen, between my cosmopolitan father from Athens and my unworldly, peasant mother from the island of Mytelene. As a child, my mother had cared for five younger brothers and sisters while her parents tended their olive groves. She'd been burned out before she'd had her first child, and was chronically depressed by the time she had me. She felt alone and abandoned in a foreign land, married to a man who did not love her and had no interest in being a father with responsibilities. She was bereft of hope, another Greek tragedy. I understand this now. I didn't then.

"Ma," I started. "It's Christmas Eve, you know. Aren't we going to even get a tree?"

"A tree?" she shot back. "What are you talking about? Can't you see how sick I am? If you weren't so selfish, you'd run to the nearest church, fall on your knees, and pray to God to give me good health."

Now it was my turn to groan. I knew her lines by heart.

"And besides," she added, shaking her finger at me from her bed, "where am I going to find the money? Your father, that *koproskilo* [rotten dog], left us penniless."

Once again, I heard what a tyrant my father had been, how he'd mistreated her, betrayed her with other women, drank, and gambled his money away. All men, she reminded me, were just like my father—no good and after only one thing. I'd find that out for myself someday, just wait.

I sat there with my mother's depression suffocating me. With my last ounce of hope, I pleaded with her once more.

"Please, Ma, let me try to get a tree," I begged. "Can't you even give me a dollar for one?"

"No," she shouted back. "Have you lost your mind? It's too cold and dark out. Besides where can you buy a tree for a dollar?"

"We should have a tree," I repeated, feeling I was talking to an impenetrable wall.

The tree now seemed tremendously important, despite the

obstacles my mother put in the way. I believed it would make a difference to the darkness of the apartment, and my life. Perhaps it would cheer the dismal place up and, by some miracle, inspire my mother to venture away from her creaking bed and get into the holiday spirit.

I went back into her bedroom and stood silently at the foot of her bed. Without speaking, she took her purse from beneath the pillow and carefully gave me a single dollar. Before she could change her mind, I grabbed my jacket and, with the dollar tight in my fist, ran down the stairs two at a time, to the street.

It was so cold I could see my breath in the winter air. The streets were deserted. A thin crust of snow had turned to ice and I walked carefully so as not to slip and fall. Everything was quiet, except for the icy wind that stung my face like needles. I dug my hands deep into my jacket pocket and fought the wind, head down.

I headed first for Union Avenue. I loved to shop there on Saturdays with my mother because the clerks were generous with their samples of olives, cheese, and fruit. But now, only one store—a produce store—was open.

"Mister, do you have any Christmas trees?" I asked, hoping he might have a few hidden in the back of his store. "Do you know where I can get one?"

"No, girlie. Don't you know there's a strike on?" he said as he closed out the till. "We ain't got none this year."

I walked on to Prospect Avenue. Then I saw two giant Irish policemen walking toward me. I stopped in front of them, feeling very small and scared.

"Officer," I began, but I couldn't say more as I choked up with tears and started to cry.

"What's the matter?" one asked.

Through my sobs, I told them.

Once again I heard, "But don't you know there's a strike on, little girl? There are no trees."

I shook my head, no. "I have to have one," I said desperately.

They exchanged looks and then each took me by the hand. We walked, checking with the last few store owners who were closing up on Prospect Avenue. Somehow I felt hopeful as we walked up and down the streets.

Late shoppers eyed me with suspicion. Their silent stares seemed to ask: What crime might this little girl have committed to be walking between two officers of the law? I began to shiver. My teeth chattered. I felt so cold that finally I, too, gave up.

What an idea that I could get a tree on Christmas Eve. My mother was right. I was crazy.

Through my chattering teeth, I turned to one of the policemen and said, "Maybe I better go home now. It's getting late."

He nodded.

As we turned to walk back, a huge truck rounded the corner piled high with Christmas trees. One of the policemen whistled and hailed the truck down. Tires screeched, and the truck came to a halt. The policeman ran over and talked to the driver for a moment, pointed to me, went to the back of the truck and took down a tree.

The tree seemed huge. The policeman steadied it for me to hold. I was stunned, in shock that the tree was actually standing in front of me. Even now, I can remember the smell of the pine and how the bark of the tree hurt my small fingers as I held onto it. I shoved the crumpled dollar in the policeman's hands, thanked them both, and ran home, half-carrying, half-dragging the tree behind me.

When I finally got home, steam was singing from the radiator, and the apartment was warmer than it had been. My mother sat up in bed, mystified. She reminded me that we only had a few tree ornaments and most of them were broken. "That's OK," I said. I searched deep in the closets until I found two dented boxes of old ornaments and used tinsel. I decorated my tree with care and, to me, it was the most beautiful Christmas tree in the world.

I wish I could say my mother smiled and embraced me, or praised me for my courage in venturing out alone. But hers was a small world of sorrow she could not escape. She'd never know how, for years, remembering that tree helped me survive not only Christmas Eve, but our desolate life.

Now when Christmas comes, bringing its memories of childhood, I'm kinder to myself. I stay close to home. I sing Christmas carols in church. When I venture out, I make a point to reach out to those friends and relatives who know who I am, where I came from, who understand, love, and accept me.

I've come to see that particular Christmas tree from my past as a part inside me with strength and courage that helped me persevere when it would have been easier to give up in defeat. The tree that night was a symbol of hope for that kid who was desperate for something to hold onto. It still is.

WATER DREAMS

Trena Noval

THE WINTER SKY IS UNRAVELING and there is water everywhere, coming down relentlessly, without reprieve. Sheets of water pour off the roof of my house. A rushing stream forms in the gully of my street, charging downhill past my front door, moving with the force of rapids, its ambition to forge a new canyon in its wake.

During this rainy season I have been daring the weather— walking without an umbrella or raincoat, letting the fullness of the water drench me if it will, out of bounds of my own good sense. Trying to unleash some sense of my own unfulfilled desires, I guess.

This morning Sam and I leave our front door and enter into the weather. He is wearing his new shoes and not his rain boots as I had asked. At eight, he cannot wait for the deluge to end for fear the novelty of his new shoes will wear off if he waits one more day to put them on. As we walk to the car, the force of the flowing stream in the gully is magnetic. I can see the language of the water seducing him: the sound of it moving, the sight of it both clear and murky, and the rippling reflections that in some places smooth out to a sheet of glass as it moves down the hill. Sam walks down the driveway and away from the car we are loading for our daily trip to school. Then, with his new shoes on, his jacket unzipped, and his orange backpack strapped to his shoulders, he steps into the rapid water and stands there hypnotized by its shearing fans. Rushing water hugs the back of his pants and tries to make its way around his feet and legs. He just stands there frozen in place, liberated from his daily routine and captivated by his own desire.

I imagine that the pure delight of stepping out of bounds into the rushing water, interrupting its rhythm, changing its pattern, and standing up to its force, is exhilarating for him. But we are late. Late getting out of bed this morning, late getting dressed, making lunch, eating breakfast, tying new shoes, late getting out the door. He begins to pick up one foot then the other, as if in slow motion at first, and then faster and faster to test the will of the water against his. I am torn. Should I pull him out, get this show on the road? Or let it go?

"What are you doing?" I ask him.

"Looking at the water," he says, his gaze still glued to his feet.

I close my eyes and turn toward the car. All right. I'll give in for a few moments. He's already soaked. In my mind I walk back up the path to the house, unlock the front door, and run through my memory of where I last saw his other pair of not-so-new but still-dry shoes.

As I load our bags into the car the rain starts again, a mist falling on my face. I am flooded with a long-ago memory of myself as a child, on a swing.

It had just rained, one of those wild Northeastern summer rains where we were cooped up in the house for hours. Then there was a short respite, the sky still dark and threatening, but my mother allowed me to go outside until the water came down again. There was a small lake under the swing where my feet touched the ground to kick off and pump. I was lying on my belly across the rubber strap seat of the swing, swinging from side to side until the gravity of my body caused a momentum that spun me in a circle. The chains of the swing twisted together like a braid, and I was suspended over this body of water like an acrobat, the swing rising higher away from the ground as the chain straps twisted more and more. Then I let go of my clockwise motion, and the chains began unraveling in reverse. I came twirling around and around, moving down faster and faster, closer to the lake beneath me with a wild speed, the ground a blur, my whole body mesmerized as my gaze was fixed on my hands and feet cutting the water like a propeller. Soaked to the bone, my hair hanging down, dragging in the muddy water like clumps of seaweed, I felt liberated by some unbound desire.

I turn to look at Sam again, his pant legs now drenched up to his knees. He is in a trance, amazed at his own power to interrupt the path of nature. I look at the water moving around him, and I am momentarily filled with that motherly angst. I want to *scream* at him to get out of the water, but I can't, unsure whether I am angry or entranced myself by the weather this morning. I look back at the car and then at Sam again and our eyes meet. He has that big, beautiful, toothy grin on his face, and I can't resist. I smile back, turning my back to the waiting car, and head down the driveway to join him on the bank of the rushing stream.

MORNINGS IN THE PARK

Martha Slavin

LAST SPRING I STARTED WALKING every weekday morning around the circular path at Osage Station Park in Danville. First I stretch against the cold, red metal fence, then I proceed past the rose-bushes that line the path halfway around the park. The roses are dedicated to past Danville citizens. At each rose bed the bronze plaques add a poignancy to my walk as I read the names of people who are just a memory now. The roses bloom profusely through spring, summer, and fall with a range of colors from white to blush-pink to deep red. A few intense plum-colored ones mingle with the others. I pass stands of sycamore, alder, walnut, and maple trees that grow next to the green playing fields in the center. Walking every day through the park has led me to realize all the small changes that occur through the year. Like a Monet painting, the park alters its colors, its light, and its activities with each season.

At 7 a.m., the park is gray, almost ghostlike. The many tree trunks are indistinct one from another; their heavy, leaf-laden branches intertwine. The only colors are the roses beneath the tree branches. Very few people walk this early. I am usually the first one there, but I am soon joined by a few dog walkers: a mother, her young teenage daughter, and their white terrier with his tail wrapped in a green bandage; an older woman with a miniature poodle, plastic bag in hand. Then others arrive: a man on a bicycle makes two circuits of the path, a woman with white hair trudges slowly around the fields, a man performs tai chi under the trees. Some people I see only once; others become familiar, and we acknowledge each other with a quick greeting.

As I walk briskly around the path, I look up to Mt. Diablo in the distance. The sun is just beginning to touch its peak with light. The mountain, like Mt. Fuji, stands out from all that it surrounds. Mt. Diablo's dark presence towers over the rolling hills that vary with the seasons, changing color from green to dusty brown. This vista of the mountain, the park's trees blocking out all signs of buildings or roads, and the large expanse of grass make the scene look like a high alpine valley.

In the summer, I walk an hour later, and the park begins to hum with activity.

Camps set up science experiments for school-age kids, preschoolers gather together and draw pictures on the path, young mothers bring their toddlers to play on the climbing structures. One week the Giants offer a baseball camp, and sons, armed with baseball gear, hustle to the field while dads, reluctant to leave, drink coffee and reminisce with each other. The next week four-year-olds try to swing plastic golf clubs. Then more baseball camps follow, and soccer camps, and a group of learning-disabled youngsters play their own game of baseball on one of the diamonds.

When fall comes, all the camps cease, and I return to my early walk. Red, orange, and yellow leaves start covering the path, as the wind blows them down. The roses still bloom. I pass the same walkers I used to see in the spring. On my third lap around the path, kids enter the park to walk to Charlotte Wood Middle School. The boys banter with each other while the girls ignore them. A group of park workers arrive and spread out to pick up trash. Another group works to clean up the playground where my son, Theo, used to play as a young child. The structures have been rebuilt, and now the teenage Theo complains that they are no longer fun, because all the danger has been removed.

As I come around for my fourth and final lap, I pass the school as the sun comes up, blinding me with its morning light. The sun casts long shadows across the fields, and the tree trunks on the other side of the grass now stand out clearly one from another. When I come around to the path's beginning, I lean once again on the red metal fence, still cool to the touch. I wonder how cold it will feel in winter.

2

OUR PARENTS, OURSELVES

PETITE MADAME

Mary Ford

THE MEMORIES that I carry of my mother have changed in the past year. Recently, the color has come up on the disappointments I've felt, and down on her small kindnesses and the sacrifices she made for me.

My mother Alice is 76, and her health waxes and wanes. One week she is vague, blue, and tired. She barks at her husband, hears criticisms of her where there are none, and plans her day carefully so that she has minimal stair trips to other parts of the house. The next week, she talks vivaciously and can trot out to the movies or for a spin to the market or hair salon, though she has to be back in four hours to breathe from her nebulizer.

Alice has emphysema, and a variable but persistent problem with alcohol. She was always someone with a sharp mind and a quick, dry sense of humor—and still is, at times. It's hard to witness her losing her bearings during conversations, or saying terrible things that she doesn't remember, even minutes later. I get angry with her for drinking. Also for smoking, even now, as she gags and gasps for breath while I talk to her on the phone. She sucks on the nebulizer tube and a cigarette, one to the other, sometimes back and forth. It's maddening and heartbreaking, all at the same time.

The whole family did an intervention with Mom last year, and she spent a full month in residential alcohol treatment. But within months she picked up where she left off, as soon as she found a lung doctor to tell her that maybe one or two drinks a day wouldn't hurt, if drinking would relax her and help her not smoke. Then she started smoking again.

I know in my heart that it is no good having more conversations about any of this; that she is, somewhere, quite mortified by this part of her life, and fights to ignore what she is doing.

I get furious with her for losing track of herself, for seeming to give up, for not letting me fix her. I know this last part about fixing is absurd, but logic trails far behind my heart when it comes to fantasies of rescue that return my mother to me.

In my mind's eye, Alice is still the meticulously groomed, well-clothed *petite madame* with knockout legs and small tapered hands. She wears rare and lush colors in muted greens, browns, and taupe, or sprays of bright colors embedded in dark backgrounds. Her jewelry is still spare and gold, and her deep-set hazel eyes still have the quality of jewels; their edges glint in soft light.

My mother's taste for her surroundings leans toward the classical, but her color schemes have always been exciting. When we moved into a large house in Maryland that had once been an embassy, she turned the pasty, drafty living room into a cavern of burnt-orange walls, with generous couches and a thick, deep-red rug. Coming home after school, the teenagers congregated here like foxes dropping into a dark den. Sometimes we spilled into the solarium to play the record player, leaning down into the wooden RCA cabinet tucked under a huge green frond, in a tiled jungle of oversize palms, ferns, rubber trees, white wingback chairs, Caribbean pastels, and brilliant sunlight. I still dream about that house; dream that I find new doors in the walls leading to more rooms, each with new colors and mysteries.

Alice was a professional-class chef specializing in Chinese food. She made S'uan L'a T'ang (hot and sour soup) and Lo Mein when that wasn't really "in" yet, and donated auction dinners of her Peking Duck to worthy causes. I remember those ducks hanging suspended in the oven, draining their fat. I'd wait and wait in a salivating trance until I could finally taste the crispy skin crackle and tear between my teeth. Other times, my eight-year-old eyes bugged out in terror as she threw together new combinations of food, though her experiments nearly always filled my mouth with glee.

Alice played and won tennis tournaments well into her sixties, giving the prized T-shirts ("CHAMPION!") to her grandkids. She competed with a wicked serve and a dominating long shot that shredded the back line. Her bridge and poker skills were so fierce and notorious that she and her partner were known as "Spite and Alice."

I remember my mother as the woman who quietly gave Barbara, my friend Melissa's mother, thousands of dollars after Barbara's husband left her suddenly and completely with two girls to raise. "I've been lucky" was all Mom said when I asked her about it years later. In the '60s and '70s, my dad was racially integrating his housing complexes, and angry people used to call our house and say terrible things. My mom would wind up one of those red-and-white chattering-teeth toys and let it laugh into the phone receiver. Mom was the one who told me that she wouldn't try pot again, because the one time she tried it, she ended up at a party telling a sugar lobby lawyer (one of the ones who got saccharine banned) that he was morally bankrupt.

When Mom found out for the second time in ten years that her husband was seeing a woman in a distant city, she kicked my father out, lost 30 pounds, got a facelift, and went on a Bali cruise with her friends for three weeks. When she came back, my father was at the doorstep with his hat in hand.

"What can I do?" she asked me. "I hate to admit it, but I think part of the reason I didn't leave him last time was because I wouldn't let his money go to that woman and not to you kids. But I can't do that again. I don't know how I feel about him or what to do." My mother broke through her confusion by telling her husband that he could immediately and irrevocably sign over half of all his assets, at which point she'd be able to decide how she felt about him apart from other considerations. It nearly killed my father, but he did it, probably with the same glint of admiration in his eyes that was in my own. They reconciled over the course of that next year. She made a remarkable leap in no-holds-barred creative thinking under pressure, as far as I'm concerned.

I miss this person who played and pushed back so lustily. She shows up now and again, but these days, I think Mom is increasingly locked in battle with her own self-judgments as she reviews her life. So, I'm purposefully recalling these Mom stories, to bring up the brightness on the good things about her to hold in my heart—and maybe bring them up with her at my next visit. I want to set aside my fantasies and meet her where she is with compassion—because of all she's been to me, and all she's given to me. And because I get to have her back when I do.

I don't want to miss out on moments that are still possible at this point in our lives. I need to remember all of who she is behind those hazel eyes.

LANGUAGE OF SILENCE

Diana Divecha

PEOPLE DON'T TALK MUCH in the small town where I am from on the north shore of Lake Superior. All Scandinavians, we are known for our reticence and remove. In fact, we are so well-known for our minimalist language and unique pronunciations (made infamous in the movie *Fargo*) that books are written on *How to Talk Minnesotan* and *Scandinavian Humor and Other Myths*. The joke circulates: "How can you tell the extrovert in a crowd of Minnesotans? He's the one looking at other people's shoes instead of his own." My own father, a hard-working milkman and woodworker with a taste for country and western, was so silent he seemed to disappear, merged with the trees in the great north woods which he sought out whenever he could. He was a man of the 1950s, conscientious, responsible, the strong silent type. If he had a free moment, he found work that needed to be done: the roof, the garage, shoveling, mowing. In my girlhood, I interpreted his distance as being checked out, unavailable, perhaps disapproving of me.

In a Midwestern way, my mother whirled around managing four children, housework, and the business side of my father's milk route. My sister and brothers were planets in different orbits. Talk was functional at best, limited to directions, news, gossip, and perhaps a joke. Lacking descriptive subtlety for nuanced experience, I felt utterly alone. I felt trapped inside my own head as the schism between the possible and the real became larger.

In school I somehow moved forward, excelled even, in areas where there was a formal structure to words: textbooks, classes, foreign languages. While I loved reading and analyzing complex thoughts, oral presentations were a fate worse than death. I managed to have leadership roles in student council, pep club, and ski club, although looking back, I wonder how I did it without expressing myself—like a long-distance runner dragging a club-foot. Perhaps my organization and strategic planning abilities helped, or maybe it was just that I was tall.

In college I was drawn to psychology, where I learned to put words to experience and entire systems of words to express a myriad of psychological realities. When I went to graduate school in developmental psychology, the linguistic expectations were a shock to my system. Words were the medium in which we trafficked. At one point I considered that I might have expressive aphasia, a neurological disorder that is an impairment of the ability to express oneself. My self-diagnosis was based on my continual frustration with my own inferior verbal fluency. So I worked hard, mining resources, collecting words, taking note of words that had resonance like "pedagogy," "psychopathy," and "efficacious." I learned the discipline of certain word arrangements in scientific writing, and the power and authority of having one's own words printed, circulated, discussed.

My best friend was an Italian woman whose words flowed freely and were peppered liberally with humor and subtlety. I dated, and eventually married, a man from India, from whom flowed a sea of words, a flood that expressed the mind, the soul, the heart, disagreement, and stories. Traveling to India with him was another shock—Indians being prone to long discourses of gossip, shouting, raised voices, interruptions, soliloquies, long tales, and raucous teasing and laughter. Initially this was so overwhelming, I'd go to bed sick with, yes, a sore throat. But inevitably I'd recover and join in, experimenting with the larger presence Indian conversation required. Though the language was more tumultuous, the loving acceptance which contained it was also more evident. Indian expressions of love were frequent and nuanced, and their timing and valence always seemed just right. The freedom to *express* myself in such complicated and changing ways meant the freedom to *be* myself.

Occasionally, when visiting my family, I needed to "code switch," shifting language systems back to Minnesotan. In contrast to my life in California or in India, the long silences of Minnesotans became glaring and I became impatient with the lack of verbal sharing. There, sitting down to talk is a formal act reserved for guests or trouble with the school principal. But how could we *not* talk, since I'd been away for so long? My urban, loquacious Indian husband took up the call to translate. "Your family may not stop for conversation, expressing verbally how they feel," he explained. "But look at their actions. See how your brother brought out his boat for you, taught our daughter to water-ski, and opened his home to us? See how your father got in the canoe with you even though his arthritic knees make him suffer to do so? You may not get the words you want, but listen to what their behavior is saying." It brought me up short. I wanted words but my family was speaking to me in a language I didn't understand. And of course the implication that I'd been misinterpreting their meaning or intention for a long time was just too much to process. I was reluctant to tune back in to an old channel that never worked for me in the first place.

But then life always presents its own insistent rhythms. When my husband was out of town for my 44th birthday, I felt sorry for myself; his absence echoed my father's for all my childhood birthdays as his deer hunting conflicted with my autumn celebration. Suddenly the doorbell rang. "You get it!" my children shouted to me in unison. I opened the front door, and there stood my dad in full red-plaid hunting regalia, complete with the fluorescent-orange Elmer Fudd hunting cap and sheathed knife dangling from his bullet-laden belt. "Seen any deer?" he twinkled. For years, he'd plotted this surprise, waiting for the right time to spring it.

There are some concepts that are too complex, too rich, too transcendent for words: He knew what I'd been struggling with, and though he doesn't speak Verbal, he turned up his Nonverbal volume to where I could hear it. And it meant, "I see you, I'm available, and I love you." Later, as he strummed his guitar in my living room or made birdhouses with my children, I read his behavior, and it said all I needed to know: that in his way, he loved me and my family. I have begun to listen with my other ear, see with my other eye.

I am now becoming conversant in Nonverbal, and am even picking up on its shades. One of the gifts of being Minnesotan is that we're comfortable with silence. In a fast-paced life, nothing restores me now like the damp silence in the woods, expansive silence in a yoga practice, beautiful alive silence in my garden. I'm finding my inner Minnesotan, my husband teases.

Visiting a friend in Oregon, I breathe in the prana of the rocky stream that rushes nearby, the towering pine trees that filter dappled light onto me, the craggy snowcapped mountains just beyond. The clean dry-leaved fall air fills and nourishes me, and nature's alchemy softens my urban consciousness. And I am filled with a longing for my dad. He is the only one with whom I want to share this quiet space. No one else offers his flannel plaid-shirted presence, his comfortable rhythm of light banter and observant silences. I long to commune with his ease in this forested space. In one of our recent phone conversations, he described the early September weather at his own cabin in the woods in northern Minnesota. "Oh, it was just gorgeous," he said. "Warm, 75 degrees, not a bug in the air. I just sat out by the fire-place in my swim shorts, looking at the lake. Geez, it was beautiful. You would have loved it." After years of translation, I now know that this wasn't a weather report. He was describing that inner space that recalibrates the psyche, balances the soul, and fills the spirit with a sweet joy, and he was sharing it with me. Out in the wilderness of Oregon, I found myself with the same quality of inner space and quiet. Now I'm grateful to my dad for passing on his silence to me. Finally, I've learned to speak his language.

THE SECRET OF LIFE IS IN THE SILVERWARE

Kathleen Faraday & Joan Stevenson

KATHLEEN WRITES: Last Sunday at St. Stephen's 8 a.m. service, I glanced down to see a Cheerio under the kneeler. I confess I was completely distracted from the sermon. I wondered what baby had dropped it, and at the same time it reminded me of a card I'd just bought that reads, "A baby is God's opinion that life should go on." Treats brought to church to distract a squirming baby now mesmerized me as I watched the sunlight shine through the stained-glass window and play upon the Cheerio. My middle daughter is studying for a fine arts degree in photography and busy with photo projects: taking 12 different pictures of a single object, different angles, varying times of day. I wish she had come with me and seen the light dancing on the lone Cheerio in juxtaposition to the cross on the altar draped in red.

I find myself looking at the world through a different lens as Wendy works on her photo projects. Yesterday, as I opened the silver polish to clean four sterling silver goblets, she said, "Stop right there, Mom." Suddenly, my random polishing project became her project—tarnished and sudsy goblets, half-polished goblets, and gleaming goblets with her reflection, camera in hand. They became rather symbolic.

Tonight as Wendy prepares a War Photography presentation, I look at the news with a question. What angle of my own lens am I to use as I view photos of the current war that is theoretically over? We each have our own personal lens and differing angles. Photos of my dad in dress uniform and one in the cockpit of his WWII bomber smile at me from my bookshelf. He was on the faculty of the Air War College during the '60s. How I wish he could share his lens, his frame of reference today. I reread the letter he wrote me after my birth explaining his absence: "Your daddy is very sorry, but it was very necessary to fight to protect your mommy and you, and keep this world a nice safe place for you to grow up in and live a normal life in, free from fear and want."

Tonight I had leftover spaghetti with my oldest daughter's family. As I left the table before the Iraq War conversation got too heated, something scrunched under my foot—a lone Cheerio.

JOAN WRITES: I sit in my office surrounded by boxes. I lost my mother in February and the awesome task of looking through her belongings and determining what I will absorb into my home and what will have a new life somewhere else has consumed many hours. The clothes were easy since we did not wear the same size, but I was struck by the fact that so many were years old. Those were the ones she wore, saving the birthday gifts for special occasions. The presents were sent to the Goodwill, many with sales tags still attached.

As my brother and I worked, we were easily distracted. We spotted an old briefcase that our father had used. We reached inside and found his New York Telephone Company identification card that was 35 years old. Later we stumbled on Mother's old wallet with her ID from the Sheriff's Department in Buffalo. Mother never learned to drive so she had no license. The photographer, better prepared to deal with the criminal element, took a picture that did that pretty lady no justice.

How do you let go when you want to hang on? Slowly we emptied Mother's small apartment, leaving to the last the tiny patio that was filled with her flowers. A box of things I could not decide on reluctantly came home with me. It rested in the corner of my office for several weeks. Finally determined to finish the task, I lifted the lid. Why had I saved these homely kitchen spoons and forks? The tablespoon was badly misshapen, a victim of years of use, and the fork's tines were bent. Why had she brought them with her when she came to California from New York? They had no intrinsic value, unworthy even of the Goodwill, but she held onto them, because they were all that was left of my grandmother's silver. I threw them in the garbage only to go back hours later and retrieve them. I reached for the silver polish and applied it with vigor. They took on a luster, not a shine.

I find myself seeking them, the spoon and the fork. I hold them in special esteem. They are a reminder of all I had and all I lost.

SHAVING

Risa Nye

CHECKING my rearview mirror at a red light on my way to work this morning, I noticed that the guy in the car behind me was shaving. Glancing in *his* rearview mirror, he buzzed the razor around his chin and neck, feeling for missed whiskers with his other hand. I wondered what it must be like to shave your face every day.

Many years ago, my dad used to shave with a mug full of soap, a short stubby brush, and a safety razor. I remember looking up and watching, mesmerized, as he brushed on a soapy beard and mustache, then methodically scraped it all off until he was Dad again. My close inspection would occasionally earn me a little foam goatee or sideburns. Pink-cheeked and smooth, he some-times splashed on a bit of the Old Spice aftershave my sister and I had given him for Father's Day. I remember standing by myself on a stepstool in front of the mirror, soaping up my own little-girl face and using a corner of a washcloth to scrape it off.

Now, as a parent, I've watched my sons experience the whole ritual and necessity of shaving. It was a rite of passage—or so it seemed to me. I delighted in my daughter's journey to woman-hood. But watching boys turn into men has been uncharted territory for a woman like me who grew up without brothers.

Suddenly, voices deepen, bodies change, beards grow, and I am not sure how much of the boy remains inside the man. What do they think about, these two young men, as they navigate the terrain of their faces every day, electric razors humming?

My dad was always particular about the way he looked; it was a rare day when he chose not to shave. He liked to dress sharp and always kept his shoes shined. He did not learn these things from his father, a Russian immigrant who once absentmindedly stuck a sock, instead of a handkerchief, into his breast pocket. In fact, Dad's dapper style might have had my grandfather's inatten-tion to such details at its source.

Even when my dad's body started falling apart at age 81, grooming was important to him. A close shave and combed hair, he used to say, made him feel like his old self, even though he knew the old self was never coming back.

From winter to spring during the last year of his life, Dad was in and out of hospitals. He suffered many indignities, experienced a lot of pain, and wept easily. One sunny day, sitting outside for the first time in weeks, he folded over, sobbing and keening, with the intense anguish of a man aware of his loosening grasp on a life he loved. Not knowing what else to do, I wrapped my arms around his shoulders and held him until his tears tapered off to a deep sigh. During those months, he often spoke wistfully about his days as a young father with two little girls who called him Daddy.

During his final two weeks, my dad was cared for at home by a wonderful attendant who kept him bathed, combed, and shaved. There was a great deal of love and care in these simple, touching gestures. In the end, they were the only things that allowed him to keep his dignity. I am left with one final memory: the feel of my dad's smooth cheek as I gave him a last goodbye kiss.

One of my sons has a bit of my dad in him—as he gets older, his face has changed shape a little and the resemblance is more apparent. I put my hand on his cheek and it feels a little rough. I smile as he says, "Guess I'd better shave."

MOTHERING MOTHER

Melanie Johnston

MY MOTHER was a native New Yorker and you could tell when you met her. She had that edge, that spirit that so many New Yorkers have. Full of life, she had deep, flaming red hair, an Irish name—Maggie McCausland—and bright blue eyes that were able to draw out anyone's innermost thoughts.

She loved to laugh, dance, eat chocolate, pretend to be famous, and argue about almost anything. She was strong in a feisty sort of way, and being a longtime New Englander, she believed she could do everything and anything herself. So it was at the end of her days, when her hair had only the faintest tint of red dye left in it and her eyes only a glimmer of the blue they once were that, to my surprise, I came to mother my mother. For even when the ravages of emphysema had weakened her so much that she could barely take one step, she was still strong.

It was peculiar, to say the least—these events that turned child to mother, mother to child. At times, it was gratifying. There was my mother actually needing my help. On the other hand, it was a bit like a hard slap in the face. Was I really this old? Was this really happening? Was I actually going to say goodbye to my mother forever?

Well, not without a fight. She gave her all to live, and I do think the only reason she tried to hold on was to protect me. Somehow, some way, deep in her heart, she was still worried about her baby, her youngest child and, perhaps in her mind, her most vulnerable. She always thought I was too sweet, too kind. And while she loved that in me, she worried that people would take advantage of my heart. So she stood behind me giving me advice to draw more boundaries, to protect my soul from those she thought might hurt me.

A few days before she left me for good, she told me how much she had loved me and the joy I had given her. She could barely talk and I could barely understand her. She was in ICU wearing a version of a Darth Vader–like mask that helped stave off the coming Niagara Falls of fluid filling up her lungs. I begged the doctor to keep it on her longer—that perhaps, just maybe, please, please, she could force this dreadful disease into submission once more and give me just a few more minutes.

The cardiologist just looked at me with a coldish glare. It was "the fourth stage of emphysema," which meant there was no hope. "Your mother should not have smoked."

"I know!" I wanted to scream. "I begged her to stop for years and years. She wouldn't have any of it. She liked to smoke." But I had no time to say such things. Back to reality, the mask was being removed. The last hope was leaving. The doctor was leaving. In fact, my mother was leaving. Moving from ICU to a floor of shooting stars—hospital nomenclature for individuals who have no hope.

As the sobs burst out of me, I tried to gain control. My mother comforted me and told me, "I want to go. It's just too hard." And so I garbled out, beneath my veil of tears, my agreement. "It's OK, Mom. If you need to go, you go. But I will always love you, and I will always be grateful for all you did for me."

And then my mother fought back the ugly disease and told me, "Don't worry, Mellie. I won't go now. Let's have a nice dinner. I'd like a little chocolate." And as I sat there sobbing and laughing into the box of chocolates trying to pick one out, she cried, too, feeling our parting intensely like best friends who will never see each other again, who will never laugh or dance or argue again.

The nurse came in and interrupted. "Why are you crying, dear?" she asked me. How was I supposed to answer a question like that one from an utter stranger who should know exactly why I was crying? In fact, the entire geriatric ICU ward was not one that was full of cheer and laughter. I'm not sure why she asked me that or what kind of an answer she was looking for. But that interruption helped sober me up, and I gave my mother her chocolate, and she smiled. Sicker than sick with only four teeth left in her mouth, she still loved a good piece of chocolate. And then I told her that I would polish her nails, brush her hair, and put on her lipstick before we departed for the land of the shooting stars. So it was that I mothered my mother.

I had just been to visit my mother only one week before she left her home for her last trip to the ICU. I hadn't had time then to wash her still-beautiful gray hair. I deeply regretted this when I returned to be with her at the hospital. I had run out of time on my visit—tried to call United and postpone my departure, but couldn't get through. I couldn't get a live human being to pick up the phone. And so after 25 minutes of circling through robot talk, I gave up and just sat with my mother accepting my fate to leave sooner than I should have. Together we decided to forgo the hair until next time. How ironic. I beat myself up for this so many times during the last week of her life that I finally thought about attempting to wash it in the hospital. But my mother's discomfort would have been too great. After all, she wasn't going dancing.

That day was not her last. But it was our last real conversation. Her physician put her on a morphine drip soon after to ease the pain, and while my mother smiled at me and would hold my hand, she was not her usual self. I would constantly tell her that I loved her, and she would nod at me and close her eyes. I was terrified that she wouldn't wake up. I would tell her that I wasn't always voting Republican just to get a rise out of her, and she would look at me with wide eyes. I'm not sure how much she understood except perhaps that I was with her, bugging her until the end.

I left my cell phone number everywhere—with the nurses at the front station, on my mother's dry-erase bulletin board, pinned to her bed. Thinking it was overkill, I mentioned to the new night nurse that my cell phone number was posted and to please feel free to call if anything went wrong. "Oh," she said, "it is? I didn't see it." I brought her into the room and showed her my numerous and obvious postings and she said, "I'm so glad you showed me. I never would have noticed."

"Well," I said, "feel free to call for any reason, any reason. I am only here for my mother, and you won't be bothering me." That was at 10 p.m. At 11:30, as I was just about to lie down, the cell rang. I raced to pick it up, thinking that it was probably a family member, but no, it was the night nurse, and she felt that I should come.

She was right. It was good that I did come. For with nails beautifully polished, dirty hair painstakingly coiffed, and lipstick delicately placed on her very thin lips, my mother left me to go dancing in the heavens and to eat chocolate at whim. Yet, as I held her hand that very last time, and despite knowing that she was almost 86, I couldn't help but wonder, why did she have to go?

No one will ever love me as my mother did. No one will ever stand for me as she did nor could I ever love anyone in the same way as I loved her. It is not possible to fill up that empty space she vacated with someone else. I accept that I am at a loss. She was the strongest person I have ever met.

But every day, wherever I am, whether I'm watching my daughter in the most well-produced school play, or my son in a very tight tennis match, whether I'm wrapped up in a great book or eating the meal of the century, I will remember my mother— her amazing spirit, her strength—and I will go on as she wanted me to, holding her hand in my heart.

MALT-O-MATIC

Christine Parsons

MY FATHER THE DREAMER called last week.

"So, how's the grad school stuff coming?" he asked.

"It's not," I answered, phone wedged in the crook of my neck. I plopped my 14-year-old daughter's still-warm jeans, now smoothed and folded, atop a stack of laundry. "They turned me down. It was a long shot anyway. They had allowed me to apply past the deadline when an unexpected spot opened up. They suggested I try again, reapply for next year's class. . . but I don't know. It was probably a nutty idea anyway."

Several months ago, during a visit to Southern California, I'd shared with him my plan to get a master's degree in nonfiction writing and to teach at a community college. We sat together in his home office. Framed posters advertising the feature movies he'd filmed over the past 40 years covered the taupe walls. A stack of Academy Award–nominated DVDs had arrived that day for his review. As a voting member of the Academy of Motion Picture Arts and Sciences, he gets to vote in the Oscars. I flipped through them and asked about his time spent teaching cinematography at USC film school.

"Teaching . . . wow. It made me happier than I'd ever been before . . . ."

His voice trailed off, his eyes closed, and he left me to revisit a place in his 85-year-old mind. I didn't want to spoil the trip, got up to tiptoe out of the room. "You should do it, honey," he said, "if it's your dream."

My father's dreams saved him at age eight, when his parents hauled him off to military school. On Friday afternoons, from his second-story dorm-room window, he watched as all the other boys, dressed in pressed olive-green St. Catherine's Academy uniforms, spotted their parents arriving to pick them up for the weekend. Family car doors opened and slammed shut. Engines revved. Radio music spilled out along with mothers' laughter and dinner plans. A parade of tires crunched along the gravel road, spitting up dust clouds that trailed out past the open iron gates.

The only child left, my father sat on the edge of his bed, its corners tucked tight. He pulled off his glasses, wiped his eyes and nose with the back of his hand, flopped down on his mattress, stared at the ceiling, and let his imagination wrap around him like a mother's arms. His parents—who lived an hour away in a Mediterranean-style Hollywood villa—didn't arrive until three weeks later, having decided that one visit a month with their young son would do.

The summer I turned ten, Dad, then in his mid-forties, sat in the Universal Studio commissary between takes for a television series he was filming, lost in thought. Although he'd become a cinematographer like his late father, he hadn't yet matched his dad's Academy Award–nominated success. He longed to break into feature films, but with nine kids at home to feed he couldn't afford to quit this show.

He spotted a chocolate malted milkshake on a waitress's tray, debated whether he had enough time to order one. His mind drifted to the commissary kitchen, to a minimum-wage guy chiseling rock-hard frozen ice cream out of a cardboard tub, knuckles raw from the effort. There has to be a better way to make a milkshake, he thought, checking the time on his dad's gold Rolex. He slid his napkin in front of him, pulled a pen from his pocket and sketched.

That night, in between gulps of his Manhattan, Dad shared his idea with me.

"I think it's a revolutionary concept," he said, explaining how tall his malt-and-milkshake-making brainchild would have to be to accommodate the refrigeration unit. I nodded, asked if he wanted another drink.

"Yeah, thanks, sweetheart," he said. "You're my sunshine girl. Do you know that?" I smiled and poured a second splash of whiskey and sweet vermouth into his highball glass and hoped he'd keep talking. I found comfort in his voice and in his studio stories, even one like this, which had nothing to do with moviemaking and everything to do with dreaming big.

I, too, daydreamed—although I never told this to my father—about living on a prairie like Laura Ingalls Wilder, with my own great expanse of land just outside my front door. Or I'd come up with a new show idea for the Skate Queens, a nickname my three sisters and I gave ourselves when we zipped along in unison on the back patio. My mind often wandered to such things during math at school. My daydreams would get me into trouble and make me embarrassed. But at home, with my dad, the imagining felt right.

Dad took the second drink from me. I pulled up a vinyl floral-cushioned chair beside him and waited for him to go on. My exhausted mother had slunk off to read or watch *Dick Van Dyke* or maybe drop off to sleep. At the end of a long day Dad's studio stories failed to hold her attention the way an issue of *Vogue* with Jacqueline Kennedy Onassis on its cover could. She had covered fashion for her college newspaper, but never talked about it until 50 years later. Perhaps she, too, harbored unspoken dreams as she instinctively jotted editorial comments about the latest trends in the margins of her magazine before giving in to sleep, leaving the dishes and care and feeding of her husband to me, her fourth child.

"See, the ice cream would pump out of a spigot, soft and ready to serve," Dad said, showing me the napkin sketch he'd saved from lunch. "Just like that—in seconds." He shook his head, taking some of the salad we'd saved for him from that night's dinner. The lettuce crunched and his jowls quivered with each bite. His hazel eyes looked off into nowhere. I could see the wheels turning in his mind. Mine did too.

In the weeks that followed he mused aloud about all the things he could do if his Malt-o-Matic hit the big time. He could quit the television series, buy a new station wagon, add onto the house, and put in a swimming pool better than our neighbors'.

"We'll have a waterfall in our pool," he said, staring through the sliding glass doors at the flat, grass-covered yard. "And maybe a high dive."

My mom called out from the laundry room, her voice muffled by the tha-thumping of the washer. "Oh Gene, for God's sake, don't get their hopes up."

I hated when she did that, just when he'd painted a picture of fun family times unlike we'd ever experienced before. I was right there with him, staring out at the yard, seeing us all splashing in the pool, playing Marco Polo at night with the deep end lit up. But the spell had been broken. "Yeah, I guess you're right," he said, turning away from our shared vision, head lowered.

I grabbed his hand, pulled him toward the watercolored rendering of his Malt-o-Matic machine. The thing towered over both of us, propped up against the family room wall. He'd had a professional designer do the artwork and had it copyrighted. The only thing left was to find some investors, have a prototype built, figure out where to have it manufactured, sign up every restaurant in the United States, collect millions of dollars, and put in a pool.

By the time spring erupted, sending the San Fernando Valley into spasms of hot pink camellias and bougainvilleas, the Malt-o-Matic had disappeared, shoved along a wall of a lightless hall closet. The health department had given it the thumbs-down. Something about temperature controls in the freezing unit.

"Sorry, kids," Dad said that summer when we asked which neighbor's pool we should borrow this time. "Guess your old dad didn't come up with such a great idea after all."

I couldn't explain that the pool didn't matter. We'd taken a trip, the two of us, to an imagined destination. The souvenirs I'd collected from the journey had nothing to do with swimming.

Now, four decades later, Mr. Imagination had tethered himself to my grad school dream, like a kid to a kite. "So what if they turned you down once," he said. "Just reapply, you'll get in."

Patting the folded clothes, I knew he wanted to be the kite, the one to soar. Closing in on 90, he soon would, in a different way. I pushed away an image of him, an ever-shrinking dot in a cloudless sky. I didn't want to lose him or his dreams.

"Thing is, Dad, I'm 52," I said, startling myself.

"What? Are you nuts? I taught people your age at film school. They did great."

I changed the subject, brought up the Malt-o-Matic. He was off and running, remembering, calculating how much money he'd have by now if only he'd held on until the fast-food craze hit.

"Hey, that was a great idea, though, wasn't it?"

Days later a new application arrived in the mail from the school that had turned me down. Holding the large manila envelope in my hands, I faltered again. Was I too old to do this now? Why had they given the open spot to someone else after encouraging me to apply? My dad's words replayed in my mind like one of those Nike ads: *Just Do It.* I picked up the phone. If I was going to reapply, I should talk to the program director, find out where I went wrong.

"Christine, oh, I'm so sorry," he began. I wanted to disappear, hang up, toss my application into the nearest recycling bin. "I don't understand why you never got word. We've already admitted you for next fall. Or you can start this spring, if you'd like."

I called my dad to give him the good news. He was napping—dreaming, I hope, about milkshakes and swimming pools, and the daughter who'd grow up to write about them all.

MA'S MANNERISMS

Sarah Weinberg

MY DAD AND I ARE EATING at a restaurant my parents frequented, the Beach Café in Manhattan, just the two of us in the smoking section. "Yes, I'll have the fillet of sole," I tell the waiter, knowing I'm using Ma's gestures. Something about the way I speak with my hands or the tone of my voice and how I form words is reminiscent of my mother's mannerisms.

I spent years fighting our resemblance. I wouldn't shop in the same fine stores as Ma did. I left New York City so I wouldn't have her New York experiences. I tried to blend in with others even though Ma always taught me to accentuate my differences. Now in spite of myself, I find that I order fish just as she did.

Especially when I'm with my father, it seems as if my mother's essence is being channeled through me. I'm sure Dad notices, because he forgets and calls me by Ma's name saying, "Helen, what would you like to order?" Then my neck and back muscles tighten.

Now I breathe in deeply the way I always do when someone is smoking cigarettes. Yes, the smell of cigarettes is comforting to me, and I really couldn't care less about inhaling secondhand smoke. Dad and I do not smoke, but Ma was a chain-smoker. So we always sit in the smoking section, perhaps out of habit and wanting to conjure up Ma's presence. A chair screeches back and forth on the wooden floor right next to us. We both turn around and expect to see Ma there ready to join us.

Ma comes over to our table and gives Dad a noisy kiss on his cheek and then one louder smack on the lips. She pulls the chair in and sits. She's wearing her watch with the paper-thin silver-linked band from Switzerland. She looks at it and says, "My train was stuck at the station and I apologize for being late." She unwraps the cellophane to her pack of True Blues and lights one up with a match. She moves her hands up and down in the air as she explains her work dilemmas. Dad and I are sitting there with blank stares. Ever since Ma went back to work full-time, as a staff analyst for the personnel division of the New York City Police Department, that is all she can talk about until she gets it out of her system. Ma loves working and her career while Dad hates his.

Dad goes to the bathroom, and Ma says, "Your father would've been content cleaning and cooking and raising you kids. He should've stayed at home, and I should've been working. We shouldn't have worried about what society expected of us."

If Dad had reached his fullest potential, I imagine he'd be sitting next to us talking about the soufflé he was going to make on Sunday after serving us poached eggs, French toast, and salmon for breakfast. Dad did a midterm in college on the art of making French toast, so I imagine him cooking lots of egg dishes. He would be happy because he'd be doing domestic chores and cooking, and not stressed dealing with numbers as an accountant. Ma doesn't like cooking much, and the only cookies, brownies, and cakes she makes are from a mix. To be fair Ma often broils us tasty steak for dinner, and I can still hear it sizzling.

When Dad returns, Ma says she finished the grant proposal she had been slaving over which shows that civilians could qualify for desk jobs in the Police Department. Some of the cops are lined up outside of her office, irate because they may lose their jobs. For a few days in a row, Ma has had to disappear so no one can find her.

While we're eating a large piece of chocolate cake for dessert with three forks, I am getting nervous. Ma's eyeing the salt and pepper shakers and the ashtrays. There have been several times now, while we're eating out, that Ma just puts them in her pocket-book and takes them. I breathe a sigh of relief as tonight is not one of those memorable occasions. She says the salt and pepper shakers are just too plain and nothing special to look at. I am embarrassed to have a mother who steals. What's more, I am afraid of my mother getting caught and feel humiliated since Ma is the one who works for the police department and therefore shouldn't break the law.

Once on vacation, we noticed that the restaurant bill looked out of whack. Dad asked the waiter why, and he explained that there is a charge for the salt and pepper shakers and the Wedgwood ashtrays; similar ones were sold in the gift shop and just couldn't be taken off of the table like that.

Tonight Ma's giving me advice again. "You know what your problem is? You're afraid of being too good at things," she says and adds, "Why do you always need to be liked by others? That's your downfall. You are not like other people. You are different. Just accept that, why don't you? Your life will be easier that way."

Then just as soon as Ma appears, she goes away, and her chair remains empty. I want my mother to come back and hold me, and I want to hold her back as I did when I lay with my arms scooped around her thin waist when she had cancer, and we took long naps together.

Now it's just Dad and I having dessert with my hands grasped firmly around the hot coffee cup for warmth in this Upper East Side café. Ma loved New York City as if it nourished her. I stayed away during many of my adult years as I did not think it healthy to conjure her up on Manhattan street corners.

"You know the hardest years you'll ever have sorting out what you want to do are the first two after college. After that it will get easier." Ma was definitely right about that one. After college I had a few jobs that did not work out. But I remembered my mother's advice, which gave me hope. And of course there was the last piece of advice Ma ever gave me, "Whatever you do, don't forget about the photography." So when we are sitting Shiva for Ma, there I am showing off and selling my photography prints to my relatives in Ma's memory. I thought about Ma's advice. Perhaps her meaning was really about me not forgetting to honor my creative side. "I will keep my life's spark alive, I promise," I say as I recite the Kaddish for my mother.

After Ma died, my sister, Martha, insisted on having our mother's watch from Switzerland.

"You have something I can never have!" my younger sister said in a loud voice.

"What's that?" I asked, stopped by the intensity of my sister's words.

"Ma's looks!" my sister said. My sister and mother were two peas in a pod snuggling, kissing, and giggling together, but I was no longer jealous of their closeness. Instead I felt sorry for all the times I teased my sister about being adopted since she didn't look anything like the rest of us.

Stunned, I relinquished my imagined grasp of Ma's watch when all I wanted to do was hold it. I wanted to feel the oil from Ma's wrists and fingers mixed in with the delicate silver links of her watchband.

"Here's the bill," I hear the waiter say, drawing me back to the present moment.

As my father and I get up to leave I look at my reflection in the restaurant's mirrored-glass wall. I see a grown-up me that looks both similar to and different from my mother. I worry a lot and my mother did not, so I think about what she used to say about my worrying. "Put all your worries on the shelf. Set your mind on your goals and go after them."

As my father and I step outside, the air is bitter cold and the wind has a bite to it. Just thinking about what my mother would have said conjures her back for one more moment. She tells me to be good and reminds me to shop in the finest stores. What she really means is for me to put my best foot forward. I think about my mother's words and move to celebrate our likeness.

WARM ENOUGH

Suzanne LaFetra

THE DAY BEFORE my mom and I were to leave balmy California, the dogsledding trip suddenly struck me as insane.

I called the Wintergreen Lodge to double-check that the XX-warm parkas I'd reserved would be ready. "And how's the weather?"

"Oh, it's warm enough for January," chirped the Minnesota saleswoman. "It's one."

One? One degree?

"Yah, I'm not even wearing a hat today," she sang in her cheerful *Fargo*-ish accent. "Yesterday was really cold, though," she said. "Minus fifty, doncha know."

Minus fifty? A full *one hundred degrees* colder than it was in my garage?

Last summer, it hadn't seemed like such a loony idea. My mom and I have always gotten along pretty well, save for some frosty stretches in my teens. But rarely have we done much together besides mothering and daughtering. I wasn't sure I was ready to break new ground—particularly frozen ground—with my 64-year-old mom.

"You're lucky," my best friend said when I mentioned the possibility. Her mom had trouble just getting through a game of golf. "Our parents are getting old," she'd said, shaking her head.

My mom and I flipped through the brochures in my sweltering California backyard. From the pages smiled apple-cheeked people petting fluffy, snowy dogs. Glistening icicles dangled from powdered sugary trees.

"This is going to be so cool, Mom," I said, fanning myself with a straw hat. "More lemonade?"

I didn't really think about the trip for a few months. I patted sand castles with my kids, carved a grinning jack-o'-lantern, and peered at columns of dark smoke when hot winds sparked autumn fires nearby.

Then, shopping for Christmas presents, it hit me: We were

going to the coldest spot in the continental U.S. in mid-January. What had we been thinking?

I flipped through a winter clothing catalog. *Sorel Caribou boots, rated to minus 40.* I ordered a pair for each of us.

After New Year's, my mom phoned me. "Ely, Minnesota is colder than Moscow today!" she was breathless with excitement. "Even Helsinki was warmer!"

I went to REI and bought super tundra-weight high-altitude mega-wimp fleece long johns. "I need the warmest gloves you have," I said to the bearded mountain guy in the green vest.

"Sure. Heading up to Mammoth?"

"Nope. Minnesota."

He stopped rummaging through the box of mittens.

"Why?"

Good freaking question.

"Dogsledding," I said. "With my mom."

He stared at me for a second. "Try these." He grabbed a package of Hot Hands, little chemical patches you slip into your gloves. I dumped the whole box into my basket.

"Nice day out there, folks," the pilot said as we taxied on the tarmac. "Six degrees with a slight breeze out of the northeast."

My mom whipped out her cell phone and called my stepdad. "We've landed!" she shouted into the phone. "There's snow everywhere!"

In the tiny airport, I saw things I'd never seen in California. A moose head hung over the drinking fountain. Past the security checkpoint a stuffed grizzly bear pawed the air with his club-sized foot.

"You the folks from California?" a chunk of a woman in a fur-lined camouflage parka said in her singsong accent.

I nodded.

"Okeydokey, then. I'm Wanda." She motioned toward the taxi purring at the curb. She hoisted my mom's suitcase. "So, you guys ever seen snow before?"

We filed out into the icy afternoon, the low winter sun glinting across the slick highway. We sped past iron mines, a store called

Chocolate Moose, and a town called Embarrass. Flakes fuzzed the windows while Wanda passed back pictures of her grandkids. She asked if we'd ever felt an earthquake.

It was three-thirty and getting dark when we arrived at the Wintergreen Lodge. "Oh, you're the ones from California," said Dominic, one of our guides. He introduced us to our fellow mushers, all from cold-weather places. One was even sporting a T-shirt.

Dominic announced we'd start Dogsledding 101 after dinner. "But first, let's talk about fears and expectations."

"Yah, then we need to go over your clothing system," said Lynn Anne, the other guide. She was looking right at my mom and me.

One woman said she was afraid she wouldn't be able to handle the dogs. Another confessed her fear of falling through the ice. My mom didn't know if her cell phone would work in negative-degree weather. I was wondering what the hell a "clothing system" was. And my feet were cold.

"Uh, I'm a little worried that my contacts are going to freeze to my eyeballs." I had read that such things could happen. I wanted to be ready.

Dominic shook his shaggy head. "If you get it in your mind that you're going to be cold, you'll be miserable," he said. "Besides, it's only 15 below."

We practiced saying "gee" for right turn, and "hike" for go. We gobbled hunks of Baked Alaska. Then Lynn Anne asked us to lay out all our cold-weather gear. She picked through our multiple fleece jackets, the Polartec leggings, the boots with extra liners.

"You guys are going to roast," she said. My mom and I beamed. People started yawning, and made for their rooms. But we were still on West Coast time and wide awake.

"Hey," my mom said, "let's see if we can see the northern lights." Her face glowed.

"You mean outside?"

"Come on," she nudged me. "We'll try out our 'clothing system.'"

"Okeydokey."

We pulled on thermals. Insulated snow pants. Then a fleece jacket. Another fleece anorak, then the shell. Two pairs of socks and two hats. The minus-40 Sorels. Glove liners and mittens. And for good measure, I yanked my neck gaiter up over my mouth. I was ready to rob an igloo.

"Mmmffphrgg," my mom said, and poked an appendage toward the front door.

Outside, I squinched my eyelids so only a nanometer of pupil was showing and braced for the icy blast. I gripped the handrail and started down, like Neil Armstrong descending. *That's one small stair, one giant step for the wimpy Californian.*

The spruce trees were like giant green toothbrushes with a foot of icy white toothpaste squirted onto their branches. We waded through the thigh-deep powder on White Iron Lake. A half moon winked from behind a cluster of clouds, bathing everything in a fairy-tale white.

My mom's breathing was heavy and I stopped. I thought of wolves. Of Robert Frost's poem. Of the ice, solid under our feet.

"I forgot how quiet it gets in the snow," she whispered. I pulled down my neck gaiter and looked up. Tiny diamonds gleamed in the black bowl of the sky. Orion, the hunter. The dog star. Polaris.

We hadn't gazed at the stars together since I was a little girl, back when time stretched out in front of us like a long summer day.

"It's wonderful to be here together, honey," she said. Her breath hung warm in the icy air.

You're lucky, my friend's words echoed in my head.

I nodded, and deep inside my ears I heard the shushing of my heart, the blood running hot and strong through my body.

My mom turned to smile at me. Well, she crinkled up her eyes so I assumed she was smiling, because I could see only a one-inch strip of her face.

And we were warm enough to stand together for a long time on that frozen lake, staring at the stars moving slowly but surely across the wintry sky.

3
COUPLES

LONELINESS

Swathi Desai

LONELINESS DIDN'T COME KNOCKING, or greet me at my window. She didn't make an appointment, or call to chat about the weather. One day I discovered her right next to me in bed. You could say that I woke up to Loneliness. She seemed to know who I was. She told me that she had grown tired of waiting for me, so she decided to take a nap in my bed.

Oh, I thought. Even Loneliness gets tired. She didn't help me make the bed even though she had slept in it. She just watched me. Loneliness can be lazy. After I noticed her in my bed, I saw her everywhere. At the dry cleaner's, at the gas station. She sat in the passenger seat of my car on my way to work. She preferred no radio in the morning, but I insisted. She just turned and looked out the window at the distant hills. I drank my coffee and listened to the morning show.

She was fond of traveling with me on business trips. She encouraged me to eat at restaurants by myself instead of ordering room service. She waited with me in the airport lounges, somberly following me down the gangway into the airplane. She sat quietly next to me in my cubicle while I worked on my computer. I offered her magazines while she waited for me, but she declined. She stared at the ceiling. She counted the acoustic tiles. She would have looked out the window, except my cubicle was without one, so I bought a framed poster of an ocean view to hang there. It was the first personal item I had ever brought to work. I didn't want my co-workers looking at my family photos, but now that I had Loneliness with me, I thought it only proper that she should have something to look at while she waited.

She was my frequent dinner guest while my husband worked late hours at the office. She was a good guest, in my opinion, because she never asked for anything. Only she never helped with the dishes, either. She stayed up with me to watch television, but she didn't think much of the shows that I watched. She preferred instead to look out the window above the television even though it was dark out. I once asked her why, but she just shrugged her shoulders and said that she connected more to the night sky than anything else. But you can't really see anything out there, I pointed out. She shrugged again, not explaining any further. She wasn't much of a talker.

When my husband started sleeping in the guest bedroom, I asked Loneliness to come sleep with me. It was the first time I had asked anything of her. She didn't ask why her, why now. She just nodded her head, got into bed on my husband's side and closed her eyes. On that first night, I couldn't tell if she was sleeping or not, so I very quietly asked her if she was awake. She turned over toward me and said that she was. Oh, I said. She didn't seem angry with me for disturbing her. Now that I had her attention, I didn't know what to say. I resorted to small talk. I asked her about her plans for the future. She asked me why I wanted to know about her plans. Thinking that she was offended by my question, possibly because she thought I wanted her to leave, I quickly added that I was in no hurry for her to leave. No? she asked. No, I said. I surprised myself. I told her that I had gotten used to her presence. She smiled when she heard that. It was the first time I had seen her smile. I knew she was smiling because I saw her white teeth glowing in the dark. That's good, she said, because she needed to stay awhile longer. I was a little confused by her answer, but maybe she needed time to collect herself. She didn't seem to have any marketable skills.

The next morning, my husband called me from work, which he never does, to ask me to meet him at a restaurant, which we never frequent. All day long, I saw Loneliness looking at me out of the corner of her eye. I was too preoccupied to ask her why. I wondered why my husband couldn't just come home and then we could change together and drive over in one car. I looked in the mirror to check my makeup one more time, but I noticed I didn't see Loneliness watching me as she usually did. I shrugged my shoulders. I was going to be late if I didn't leave now.

I got into the car and drove to the restaurant. Halfway there, I noticed Loneliness wasn't beside me. It was too late now to go back for her. Oh, well, I thought. Maybe she's got more important places to go to tonight. I had to drive around the block several times to find parking. Had I just used the restaurant's valet service, I could have been on time, but I remembered that my husband frowns upon valet service as a waste of money and an unnecessary indulgence. Finally I found parking and started half-running, half-walking to the restaurant. My husband hated it when I was late! When I got there, my face was hot because of all the rushing I had to do to be on time. The hostess walked me over to my husband while I caught my breath. He, of course, had been on time and was waiting for me. The hostess pulled the chair out for me. I told him that I had difficulty finding parking and stammered something about going as fast as I could in high heels. He looked at my flushed face and asked me why I didn't just use the valet service. At that moment I wished Loneliness could have heard him. She would have raised her eyebrows, I know. I pushed his remark aside and decided to focus on the menu.

We ate our meal and I managed to enjoy it. I kept looking around the restaurant for Loneliness, but there was no sign of her. I focused again on my husband, because he seemed to be looking at me and saying something, but it was difficult to hear him. I saw his lips moving, but the few words I understood were not making any sense. He was talking about how I would be fine. I nodded, yes, of course, I would be fine, but what was he saying? He said that he had made provisions for me. Provisions? Like in the army? Or was that rations? Soon, everything was moving in slow motion like when you're trying to run under water.

He said that he had been very lonely and needed more. These words I heard. These words I knew. He said Lonely! I knew Loneliness. I said this to him. I must have said it to him because he looked at me oddly, as if I had developed a sudden speech impediment. Lonely! I said again. He leaned toward me and whispered for me to calm down. I told him I was calm. I had to make him understand! I wanted him to know that I knew Loneliness, too. And if he knew her, then maybe we had something more in common than just our marriage. He shook his head. I could see that he had been practicing. This was a speech that he had been practicing. Maybe even in front of a mirror. He continued to shake his head and say something about how it was more than loneliness. It was a, it was a . . . he kept stumbling on this last sentence. Just what was it? I asked him. He looked embarrassed by my question. He looked around the room and said that things sometimes happen. I looked behind me, half-expecting something to happen as if on cue. People we never expected sometimes come into our lives, he said. Sometimes the timing is just not right, but we have to take risks. Be open to possibilities.

I lifted my glass to my lips and took a cool drink of water and felt it move down my throat into my chest. I understood now. I set down my glass on the white linen tablecloth and looked up at my husband. Yes, I said, nodding. Sometimes people do come into our lives and we just have to make room for them. Sometimes whether we want to or not. At this last remark he looked shocked, and then relieved. His lips started moving again, and he stammered, "So you do understand! I just didn't expect you to, oh, I . . ."

I got up from the table and put my napkin down. As I gathered my belongings from the chair, I caught a glimmer of someone out of the corner of my eye. There she was standing at the door, waiting for me. I looked one more time at the lonely man sitting across the table from me. "I have to go now. Someone's waiting for me," I said as I walked toward the exit.

SAME TIME NEXT YEAR

Elizabeth Fishel

MY HUSBAND AND I GOT MARRIED in a glorious mountain retreat on a fall foliage-flecked afternoon. We stood beneath a canopy of tawny leaves, shared our vows before family and friends, and floated through a lavish meal without tasting a bite. The date was October 13th and a Friday at that, a day that gave other couples the jitters but turned out to be lucky for us. From that year on, mid-October became our own private celebratory season, and for the first few child-free years of our marriage, we marked it with a weekend away to celebrate and renew our vows.

But when one baby boy and then the second finally came along, after six years and two heartbreaking miscarriages, we were too giddy with excitement, too doting and possessive to leave them overnight. For several years we took a hiatus from our anniversary getaways, tucked the boys in on October 13th, and considered ourselves unbelievably lucky to have them. Then, usually pajama-clad and sleep-starved, we toasted each other with a glass of champagne and called it a night. "You can do anything amorous you'd like," I'd joke to my husband as we tumbled into bed, "so long as you don't wake me."

As the honeymoon of new parenting eventually gave way to the demanding dailiness of the long haul, as our babies became boys, weaned and verbal and sometimes even with plans of their own, we felt ready to revive our tradition. We yearned to be the soul mates we once were, the companions who hiked and biked together, cracked jokes and whispered secrets to each other, dawdled over a leisurely dinner out, dashed off to a late movie, and returned not too weary to keep our romance alive. But had our hyperfocus on our sons swept so many things under the rug that we'd need a month's vacation to find them? Simply carving out one night away was a formidable task. The marching orders we left behind for our babysitter rivaled the plan for the invasion of Normandy.

Sure enough, we were so distracted as we headed off, we forgot to put my suitcase in the car. So most of our precious time alone was spent restocking the essentials that we'd left behind. But since that rocky start, our anniversary night away has become an oasis in the helter-skelter of child-raising, a well from which we drink deep enough to replenish us for the rest of the year.

The place that has become "our place" is a bed and breakfast inn on the craggy coast a mere hour or so away from home. Yet its magical tree-house structure complete with redwood decks and turrets and ferny, fairy-tale landscaping transports us to another kingdom. Here, as the fire sizzles in the huge stone fireplace, gentle music hums on the stereo, and a cozy bed plumped high with quilts and pillows awaits us, we slowly turn back into the people we used to be before we got derailed by diaper changes and midnight feedings, by school meetings and soccer games. Here we sink gratefully into pampering and self-indulgence—hike for hours along the coast, soak in the hot tub under the stars, eat by candlelight, sleep blissfully late, and wake to steaming coffee and mouth-watering muffins, fruit, and frittata—made and served by somebody else. We take stock of the past year, give voice to our dreams, and help each other make decisions long deferred—to start a new job or a new book, to move or stay put, to travel East or West. Dilemmas that bothered us all year seem to unravel effortlessly with leisure and the tart sea-salty air. And of course we chatter about our children—savor their accomplishments, troubleshoot challenges lurking on the horizon—with the luxury of being uninterrupted by them. Refreshed, we return happier partners, better parents.

Recently two friends who are therapists invited us to a weekend workshop geared to long-married parents who might benefit from some professional retooling. But we declined the offer gracefully, knowing that in the magical, otherworldly splendor of our yearly overnight away, we had created our own special marriage-renewing ritual.

SATURDAY NIGHT SEDUCTION

Janis Mitchell

THE ADORED CHILD IS AWAY for the whole night so we can use the entire house. We will be free from our hypersensitive awareness of her 14-year-old self too nearby and too well able to hear and attach meaning to the sounds we make together. This gives us an uninhibited opportunity for seduction and romance. When we learn she will be on a sleepover we eye one another discreetly and start to make plans. The refrigerator is fortuitously stocked with salmon fillet, a tight little ball of Boston butter lettuce, asparagus, and a bottle of very good wine. We drop the Adored Child off at her friend's house and spring into action. I wash the lettuce and spin it in the drainer, then wrap it in a clean dishtowel to chill in the fridge. I get out the old favorite wooden salad bowl and put in a scant half teaspoon of Dijon mustard, a shake of salt, two to one of olive oil and Cabernet wine vinegar with some sliced garlic to infuse for a while. John comes up behind me and nuzzles my neck with sweet kisses. I lean against him and we sway.

When we let each other go John walks outside to fire up the barbecue. He has taken a cedar shingle left over from the resurfacing of the facade on our old Berkeley Craftsman house. He has soaked the shingle in water. He will put the salmon fillet on it before it goes on the grill to smoke and bake and absorb amazing flavor. He has carefully selected the music. It is soft jazz by Tony Bennett and Bill Evans. We keep stopping in our preparations to hold each other and indulge in long and lingering kisses. Our bodies fit so well together after 28 years, and our erotic history has so suffused our senses that we are aroused just being close together and smelling one another's skin.

John comes in from outside and approaches me with a single rose from his lovingly tended garden. It is perfectly formed, lavender colored, and fragrant with voluminous overlapping petals. He looks at me and I get the reference. He is reminding me of the afternoon a few years ago when we pulled the petals off of the flower and scattered them in our bed. We rolled around and crushed them, they stuck to our skin and released their perfume in the room and on us.

I resume preparations and snap the asparagus one piece at a time at its natural breaking point, then line up the spears on a baking sheet coated with olive oil. It goes in a hot oven to roast. Midway through the cooking I will sprinkle breadcrumbs and finely grated Parmesan over the surface. The fire outside has stopped smoking and the coals glow with readiness. We are holding each other again in the doorway. I look at the grill and I ask, "So, are we ready to start cooking yet?"

John says, "We have to eat first."

We look at each other and start to laugh, enjoying the flirtation. We dance a little, we chat a little, we enjoy our wine and the music we fell in love to way back in the '70s. Maybe we will fill up the "Tea for Two" bathtub and stretch out on opposite sides with our feet next to each other's heads. Can't hear the music in there but the lights will be low, the scene will be sensuous, and we love to look across the bathwater. Our faces appear young in the diffused light. Not that it matters. I don't see gray hair and fine lines, I just see John and I know he just sees me. We have been in love for such a long time.

A GIRL'S BEST FRIEND

Karen Yencich

MY STOVE DIED.

The electrical panel that governs the oven shorted out, and the replacement part was fabulously expensive. A new stove was in order, and after dinner one evening, parked on the sofa watching the news while my husband read the paper with my feet propped up against his legs, I reported on costs.

"Wow!" he exclaimed, impressed but not really engaged in the conversation—he has no idea what things cost, and he knew we'd get the stove anyway.

"Not really," I replied, "a diamond ring is much more expensive," offering a useful point of comparison.

His eyes snapped into focus, and I felt a lurch of alarm against my stocking feet. Without changing his outward demeanor in any way, he was suddenly alert, the way husbands are when they suspect they may be in trouble, but don't want to give too much away, just in case it's nothing after all.

"Did you want a diamond?" he asked, genuinely surprised. It was clear that it had never crossed his mind that I might want a diamond ring, and that this might have been a serious oversight.

Setting aside for the moment whether or not people should have diamond rings, or how much money is appropriate to spend on a range, his instincts had been correct. I didn't want a diamond ring.

When we got married, we were both established professionals. It was unseemly to expect my parents to pay for a wedding, so money that might have otherwise been spent on a diamond was spent on a wedding, a gift to our families. Later, I might have gotten a diamond for our first anniversary, but we went out to dinner instead. In Paris.

After that, my husband went back to graduate school, an expensive one, and our daughter was born. Then we bought a house. Then our son was born, and I quit work to stay at home with our children. The next thing we knew it was time for elementary school in a lackluster school district, and we were forking over tuition for one kid, then two. Out of respect for the earthquake fault that runs along the end of our block, we bolted the house to its foundation and added shear walls. The washer croaked. The floors had to be sanded.

We'd always loved wisteria vines, so the next time we pulled ahead financially, we built a splendid deck with a trellis for a wisteria.

By the time we'd been married 20 years, we'd run through two minivans and a secondhand Datsun. We'd trekked to the grandmas in Nebraska and Seattle dozens of times. We'd gone to every national park we passed, and once each to Disneyland and Washington, DC. For our twentieth anniversary, Grandma came over, and we went out to dinner again. In Rome.

If it sounds as if we weren't thinking about diamonds, you're right.

When I was single I was vain about my hands. My nails were always perfectly done, and I had dozens of clever, if not expensive rings to show off. If I had wanted diamonds, I could have easily purchased them myself, and thought nothing of it. But even in those days, I never wore rings on my left hand, and when I put on my wedding ring, I took off the others. I never wore them again.

My wedding ring is nothing fancy, just a narrow gold band with a milled edge. And I think, maybe because marriage is such a complicated thing, a simple ring is best. As a symbol, it reduces the circus of life to the virtues that can sustain a couple over the long haul—honor, grace, fidelity—the qualities that bear love aloft and over anger and impatience, weariness and misunderstanding, and the slings and arrows of outrageous fortune.

When the ring was new, I loved to catch its gleam out of the corner of my eye. In its simplicity, it seemed so elegant and adult. Wearing it appealed to the best in me, and I didn't take it for granted yet. I didn't know then that our individual orbits would sling us both nearer and farther from one another in the apogee and perigee of events, or how the specific gravity of children and circumstances would distort our trajectories. I didn't know that there'd be times when only loyalty to the idea of marriage would carry us over until I could remind myself that the same sweet person I had fallen in love with was at the heart of the much more interesting man who is still my husband.

Diamonds are so very fashionable now. But fashion is something you adopt for a season. Style speaks to the larger issue of those things we wear year after year because in some essential way they reveal who we are, our preferences and loyalties. My wedding ring has style, and I'm betting that it will still look good on an old woman.

So if, as common wisdom suggests, bread is the staff of life, then I definitely prefer the stove; you can't bake bread with a diamond. And while Marilyn Monroe was smart to bank on high-quality gemstones in matters of the heart, I don't think I need them; I already have a best friend.

JUNEAU

Kristine K. Mietzner

MY TALL 14-YEAR-OLD SON Ben and I were on one of the many trips the two of us have taken since his father and I divorced a few years ago. On a rainy July day, we climbed the gray-black marble steps of the Alaska State Capitol in Juneau and freely began roaming its halls. We set about to see each floor, astonished that no guards, no metal detectors, no visible security measures prevented us from visiting any part of the state house, as if 9/11 had had no impact on the place. I felt completely at home, as familiar with this building and the town as I was 20 years earlier, when I worked there as a broadcast journalist, and Ben's future father served in the governor's cabinet as the head of a state department. Ben seemed energized by the lack of restrictions and seeing for himself some parts of his mom and dad's past.

Searching for the press room, we checked the second floor. I showed Ben the large room that had been the press headquarters when I worked there. The room was located in the middle of the action halfway between the House and Senate floors, convenient for reporters covering the legislature. No longer for press, the space had been transformed into an ornate hearing room named for the late Democratic state senator Betty Fahrenkamp, her huge portrait filling much of one wall. My mind slipped into the past, the time zone in which Betty and her staff had been good friends with me and my soon-to-be husband. I remembered her hard work for good causes, her easy laugh, and the way she sometimes brought both her current and ex-husband to the same social events. I said to Ben, "Your dad and I knew her. She was a good person."

We continued exploring and encountered a custodian. "Where is the press room?" I asked. We laughed when we followed his directions and found it in the farthest corner of the building's basement. We took the stairs back to the second floor to see the House and Senate galleries and to the third floor to see the doors to the governor's offices where Ben's dad had spent many hours.

I had not returned to Juneau in the 20 years since I walked those steps while working as a reporter, producer, and co-anchor for a statewide television broadcast on the daily machinations of the Alaska State Legislature. Then I was at the top of my game professionally. I had yearned for years to have the job of covering the state legislature, and I was doing just that—considered one of the best reporters in the state.

By the end of the legislative session, I was married and pregnant with Ben's older sister and living in Juneau with my husband. When he was fired from his job in the first year of our marriage, I was seven months pregnant. I sought work in television and was offered a job as a documentary producer at the public television station in Anchorage. I turned it down to be free to follow my husband's career which was taking him back to being a city manager, this time with a job offer in California.

Again, I shook away the memories and tried to explain to my son about my decision, my choice to have children so many years earlier. At a certain spot on the stairwell landing between the second and third floors, I called Ben over to my side. He may have thought I had some particular object to show him, but instead it was simply a true story of what had happened in my heart at that particular place.

"This is the place," I told him. Pointing first at my feet, then up the stairs and out the large multipaned window, I said, "I stood right here, looked out that window, and saw the children playing outside that building. Back then it wasn't the Terry Miller State Office Building, but an elementary school, Capital School. I heard the children playing, and I decided I definitely wanted children in my life. This is where I decided to have you and your sister."

Ben patiently listened and smiled. He didn't say much, but he listened closely as I shared this revelation with him.

"That's cool."

In retrospect, it was not an amazing coincidence that I quickly became engaged after this insight about wanting children. At the time I saw myself falling in love and wanting to start a family. I set out to find a good provider and someone with some intelligence. I was a woman on a mission. With Mark, I found the qualities I sought and little else. He was a man with a good-looking suit and a good job.

Ultimately, in my view, he did not have the inner resources to stay with the marriage, and he left me. The end of the marriage brought many dark and questioning times for me. Eventually, I faced the fantasies that both my husband and I had brought to the relationship. I reflected on our roles in the good and not-so-great days of our marriage and the many problems that led to its demise. I found compassion for myself as my understanding of the past increased through counseling, attending a support group, and writing. Although I could focus on any number of faults in my ex-husband, I have learned that it's productive to remember the moments of joy.

We each own our own karma. For the sake of my children, in their presence I try very hard to speak only of their father's more positive attributes. These days I make one of two comments when my children seem to expect me to say something about their dad, the man who left me after nearly 17 years of marriage. "Your dad is an excellent provider," I say, or "Your dad is very intelligent."

In planning my trip to Juneau with Ben, I had anticipated that this particular location, the state capitol, would be the most difficult for me to navigate emotionally. I worried that I would face a lifetime of regrets on this path that might tear at my heart as though I were driving down a war-zone road filled with hidden explosive devices. But my fears fell away unrealized. As I explored the places where I had made life-changing choices as a younger woman, I learned a thing or two about myself. I walked out of the capitol feeling like the winner of a race who had just taken a victory lap.

In the familiar cool, damp drizzle of Juneau's mild summer weather, I felt comfortable with my son and my life. Like rain falling off my back, I shed the bitterness I had harbored that my ex-husband had kept me from following my dreams. I came to understand that even though the marriage didn't last, I lived out my dream of having children, and now I was free to face new challenges. No one had forced me; rather I consciously chose to start a family and temporarily leave full-time work as a journalist.

The light July rain continued falling. I felt as comfortable with my life as with the soft layers of my clothing: a blue rain jacket, gray sweater, khaki pants, and walking shoes. My long brownish-blond hair was loosely tied back. That day I embraced my life as one made up of decisions that I had made on my own.

ROMANCE IN WINTER

Marian Magid

"WHERE SHOULD WE HIKE TODAY?" my husband wondered aloud on the first day of our winter getaway in Inverness, California.

It was an ordinary question, but it magically dissolved the individual cocoons Albert and I sometimes live in at home as we pursue our separate work and interests.

We were sitting in front of what our motel's brochure called a "fireplace"—actually a black gas stove with fake logs, straight out of a 1950s Sears catalog. Albert unfolded the Point Reyes National Park map, and my eyes immediately fastened on an area we'd never explored before: the Palomarin Headlands. Tracing my finger along that trail, I touched a splash of blue labeled "Bass Lake."

We both smiled. That was *it*—the place we had to go. Why? Because 46 years ago, we had vacationed at another Bass Lake, in Southern California. Our friends, the Zimmermans, were supposed to join us, but one of their kids got sick at the last minute, so we went alone. Nine months later, our son Daniel was born.

So, it seemed provident to visit *this* Bass Lake—though the outcome would clearly be different this time.

"The sky's really overcast," Albert noticed, looking out the sliding-glass window of our room, "and the forecast is for heavy rain and high winds."

We exchanged the kind of look that needed no words after nearly 52 years of marriage. The look said, "So, what if it rains—we're tough. Let's go."

As we drove south, the sky brightened, making a dry or misty walk at least a possibility. Apparently few others read the heavens so optimistically. There was only one other vehicle in the parking lot at the trailhead, a muddy Jeep with a kayak strapped on top that looked as if it belonged to rugged outdoor guys.

The trail was deserted—all *ours*. We climbed a narrow stretch lined with thickets of baccharis bushes, their desiccated leaves giving way to tender leaflets and pregnant buds, ready to burst at the first spring sunshine. The scent of eucalyptus surrounded us; bright green grasses sprouted beside the trail.

We turned a bend into a sudden jet of wind, a gift from the ocean that roiled at the foot of the steep cliff below us. My baseball cap flew down the trail, and as I retrieved it, a new gust tried to snatch it from my hand.

Another one of those wordless looks passed between us as we scanned the view. It said, "Marvelous—gorgeous—how lucky we are to be here!" In those looks, I feel sure Albert didn't see my graying hair or my wrinkling neck. And I didn't see his nearly bald head, his hearing aids—or his occluded arteries. We might as well have been at that first Bass Lake. We were ageless and excited to be alive.

As we turned inland and climbed a bluff, my eye caught three spots of bright pink on the hillside—geraniums, not woodsy geraniums, but what looked like perfect garden or greenhouse geraniums. A mystery! A bit further, one lone yellow-orange mimulus danced in the wind, and yet further, three pink morning glory flowers bloomed on an *afternoon* in *January*.

Two guys came toward us on the trail—maybe the Jeep owners. One was well-muscled and sociable, the other thin and quiet. They wore matching REI windbreakers over T-shirts—quite a contrast to our multilayers of wool and down! The talker said they were celebrating his 50th birthday, and he was pleased that he could still hike at that age. This time our look said, "50—he's just a *kid*."

Along the next stretch of trail, perfect, plump pine trees rose incongruously out of the scrub. Then the path veered sharply, revealing a pond or lagoon at just about the place marked "Bass Lake" on the map. It was pretty, but a little disappointing, not what we'd expected.

Could it be that this wasn't the spot we were headed for? "Let's walk a little farther, even though it's starting to rain," I urged. But Albert didn't need any urging.

Less than a quarter mile down the trail, a large tree-rimmed lake suddenly came into view and stopped us with its beauty.

Could this be it? Our destination? We walked around the

perimeter of the water to a meadow. Between the field grasses and the shore foliage, a small almost-hidden sign read "Bass Lake."

This time our looks melted into a gentle kiss.

We turned and walked hand in hand, back down another part of the trail we've shared for five decades.

MOVING OUT

Leah Fisher

I WAS HOME BY MYSELF, my workday over; it was almost 10 p.m. I had eaten dinner alone. My husband was working late again.

This pattern of Nate's long workdays, late evenings at the office, and even later nighttime professional meetings has been an ongoing source of friction in our life together. A woman friend and I used to wonder—only partly in jest—if Nate had a secret, second family. But aside from the perpetual collision between Nate's ambitions and my dreams about family life, we have a good marriage. Nate is an attentive and eager listener; we have a strong friendship, a satisfying sex life, and we understand a lot about one another.

Our home life, however, even when the children were young, never felt very homey, and my disappointment remained undiminished. I missed my husband, and I yearned for him to spend more time with us. I also wanted him to be more engaged with home and homemaking. Over the years, I had tried to influence him by way of polite requests, pleading, anger, resentment, nagging, idle threats, crying, and getting depressed. None of it resulted in change. In the end, I settled into part-time work and hired loving, nurturing caregivers to help us make a warm home for the children.

When our children left for college, I fell into an immense chasm of loss. First there was the concrete loss of their company, their humor, energy, music, friends, and even their clutter. But there was also the loss of future possibility. I had to permanently let go of the hope that someday Nate would cut back his hours so our family could enjoy leisurely evenings together, so we could achieve the cozy, nurturing, homey home I had always wanted.

But neither Nate nor I had much expertise in creating such a home. Nate was totally absorbed in his work. I too was more interested in outside things. A chance for a swim, a bike ride, or a walk with a friend always seemed to trump pulling out a cookbook and trying a new recipe. Nevertheless, I certainly noticed when all the lights in our long hallway had burned out. Nate, however, maintained an uncanny ability to ignore the dark hall for weeks, even though changing lightbulbs was one of his few domestic responsibilities.

On this particular evening, I was at the computer, longing for a household where dinner was a shared event and an evening together lasted longer than the 45 minutes between Nate's return and our going to sleep. On a whim, I clicked on Craigslist, the online bulletin board for anything and everything. I looked up "roommates wanted" and read a few ads for house shares. . . too scary. Next I looked up "short-term rentals in shared houses" and found this ad:

"Come share our sweet, cozy Berkeley home filled with house-plants, altars, music, and incense. We love to cook, do yoga, and garden. We are 25- and 27-year-old women. One of us is a yoga teacher and bodyworker; the other works for a nonprofit doing youth philanthropy. We are looking for a 20-something woman or gentle man to join our warm and happy household for a month or longer. E-mail and tell us about yourself."

My heart started racing. Among my favorite and most joyful activities are gardening, singing, yoga, meditation, and massage. A month-long sublet would involve no ongoing obligation. It could provide the perfect experiment. I could find out if my fantasy of people spending an evening together, sharing cooking and eating, and making a home beautiful was just that—a fantasy— or if it might indeed fill the gaping hole I felt so often when I returned to our empty house.

Without a second thought, I shot back a reply:

"I too love altars, houseplants, meditation, yoga, incense, and gardening. I am quite interested in a one-month sublet in your cozy communal household. However, I am not 20-something. I am 59. I am married with a husband who works long hours. I would like to have company the 3-4 evenings a week that he works late and I'd like to explore ways to make our home life more fun.

P.S. Before you freak out about my age, please consider this: if all goes well, someday you will feel very much the way you do now, only you will have wrinkles and others will see you as old."

After several days, no answer. Well, I wasn't exactly surprised. Besides, it was just a late-night impulse. Still, it made me feel a little sad to realize how age can create such a barrier.

More than a week later, I received an e-mail from Serena, saying that she and Colleen had been intrigued by my response and would like to meet me. After work the next day, I drove into Berkeley for my "interview." A beautiful, doe-eyed, dark-haired young woman answered the door. This was Serena. She led me through the plant-filled, futon-furnished living room toward the kitchen. There I met Colleen, as blond and adorable as Serena was dark and exotic. They offered me tea and we chatted quite comfortably.

Of course they were extremely curious to know why I wanted to live in their house since I already had one of my own; they wondered about the state of my marriage. I assured them it was fine. I explained that it had been decades since I'd lived communally, that my husband and I had discussed the possibility of housemates. But before proceeding, I wanted to find out if my memories of collective living were romanticized or real. I also told them that I wanted my husband to experience firsthand what it was like to be the one returning home to a dark and empty house.

My explanation made sense to Serena and Colleen. Both of them had boyfriends, and they appreciated that Nate and I continued to negotiate our relationship after so many years of marriage; they also admired my ingenuity. At the end of our visit, they warmly invited me to move in.

The next evening I told Nate I had something important on my mind and wanted to talk. I explained that I was planning to rent a room for a month in a group house so that, on the nights he worked late, I could enjoy the company of housemates and see what I could learn about making our own life feel cozier.

Nate was speechless. In all the years I've known him, I have never seen my husband at a loss for words, but he was now. When he finally collected himself, he said, frostily, "Are you leaving me?"

"Absolutely not," I answered. "This is really just what I said. Any night you come home at dinnertime, I'll be here. I'll be here on the weekends. And my housemates say you are welcome to come by and to stay over any night you want."

"Do you still love me?"

"Absolutely. This isn't *against* you, Nate; it is *for* me. I'm trying to figure out how to get happy." Nate said nothing more and soon we went to bed.

At four o'clock in the morning, Nate awakened me, angry. "I am intensely upset," he said in an accusatory voice.

"Don't try to scare me with your anger," I replied, feeling threatened, but trying not to let it show.

"I'm not angry, I'm upset. Guys can sound angry when they are upset, and I am extremely upset. What you told me tonight has me *extremely* upset."

I lay on my side of the bed, silent for a long time. Then I spoke to him, quietly and carefully, but firmly. "I am finished with ignoring my needs and my dreams in order to protect you from your intense feelings. I am *so* finished with it, Nate." Nate was silent; I rolled over and went back to sleep.

I moved into my room at the Blake Street house the next Monday evening, the middle bedroom on the second floor. It already had a futon bed, a little nightstand, and a dresser. I loaded my car with some bedding, a small rug, and a favorite reading lamp (one I made in my early twenties from a brass hookah I'd found at a flea market). I brought a little wooden meditation altar (a childhood carpentry project made for me by our son), my journal, some candles, incense, a framed watercolor, and a piece of orange batik fabric to hang over the windows. These plus some toiletries and a change of clothes were sufficient. They neatly filled my station wagon.

Serena and Colleen and Serena's boyfriend, Arturo, helped me unpack my car and set up my room. I found a single white lily in a tall vase on the dresser, a welcoming gesture. After I unpacked, the four of us settled into the kitchen. It was small and plant-filled. The stove and refrigerator looked to be 50 years old; the linoleum floor looked even older. Serena and Arturo ate dinner; Colleen and I drank tea. We laughed and talked playfully, getting acquainted. It felt so sweet. What was striking, besides the friendly banter and inclusiveness, was what was missing. There was no TV in sight and no computer. The phone rang only once all evening and went unanswered. No one jumped up to check e-mail, do paperwork, or prepare for the next day. The action takes place in this house, I thought, not primarily outside it.

We wished each other good night and went upstairs. Just as I was settling into my comfortable bed to sleep, snuggling under my soft yellow flannel sheets and my daughter's down quilt, the house started shaking. Earthquake! Not in this rickety two-story house. I wanted to shake things up, but not to die! These old boards are probably termite-infested. Is a house this old even bolted to the foundation? The house shook gently, rhythmically. Gradually I recognized the motion for what it was—the rhythm of young lovemaking! I smiled with relief. In about ten minutes there was silence.

After my first night there, I spent an afternoon at home dealing with bills, arranging for home repairs, responding to messages. I enjoyed a few minutes weeding the garden in the sun, then hours indoors. I thought about the serene simplicity of my sparsely furnished room in Berkeley. I am overwhelmed at home— trapped inside my house by all the details of sustaining and main-taining it. Soon the afternoon is gone.

Talking to Serena a few evenings later, we agreed that the antidote is to set clear boundaries, to be selective, to protect home and evenings as a sanctuary. Unfortunately, I am not very disciplined about this. When Serena and Colleen get home at night, whether at 7 p.m. or 9 p.m., they are home. No more work. It is time for relaxation, conversation, music, and preparation for rest.

Friday, I returned home to Nate. We were together for three nights. I remained loving, cheerful, and fully available to him. Gradually he was starting to believe that I was not trying to punish him or "get even." He didn't ever ask about my "other home" and declined all my invitations to come by or sleep over. But at least he wasn't angry, prickly, or defensive.

One night I entered the Blake Street house to find Colleen giving a massage to a friend in the living room. The aroma of scented candles and fragrant massage oil and the glow of candle-light were embracing. In this household there is such a focus on physical well-being—healthy eating, lovely plants and flowers, music, massage. I realized that I want a life that gives more care and tenderness to our physical existence. We won't have our bodies for that much longer; I'd like to cherish and relish and celebrate them now.

The month flew by. Sometimes I found it inconvenient to go back and forth from house to house. But mostly, I enjoyed my cozy, simple, sensual times on Blake Street. I appreciated the amenities at my own house where everything is clean and well maintained. I enjoyed Nate's company when he was at home. Mostly I savored not having to spend endless evening hours alone in a big, empty house.

As my month drew to an end, a permanent renter still had not been found. Happy with my arrangement, I proposed staying on for a few more weeks. But the experiment ended abruptly on the Wednesday evening of my first "bonus" week when Serena said they were having a second interview with a young man who would like to move in immediately. He was Asian, gentle and easygoing. We all liked him fine. He had just arrived in town and had no place to sleep that night. I explained that I happened to have two places to sleep, and offered to vacate my room. So, just as quickly as they had helped me unpack and settle into my room five weeks before, my housemates helped me repack, and I was home by the time Nate returned from work at 10 p.m. He was surprised to see me, but by now, he was getting used to surprises.

Serena e-mailed me from her work the next day: "It felt empty in the house after you left. I found myself looking forward to seeing you yesterday, then poof! Everything had shifted."

It was an abrupt ending for me as well. I was left to distill what I had learned.

I learned that, although I am no longer 20-something, I can still have fun. The twenties are a juicy, delicious time of life, a time of traveling light and exploring. How wonderful that my children are smack in the middle of it. How wonderful that I can still explore and have fun too.

I learned that I have a lot of chutzpah!

I learned that Nate can give me a long leash, even when he doesn't like my ideas.

I learned that, for me, an important ingredient in having an adventure is the knowledge that I will be returning to my husband at the end of it.

I discovered how much more of my unhappiness at home results from the avalanche of paperwork and busywork rather than actual loneliness for Nate. I miss *me* at home as much as I miss my husband.

Finally, I learned how much my image of a homey home has to do with attentive care and nurturing of our physical bodies. I want to make our home a place where bodies can be protected from overstimulation and competing demands. I want home to provide us with rest and pleasure for the senses: delicious healthy food, lovely scents, inviting music.

Shortly after this experiment, two changes occurred. First, Nate announced that he had modified his work schedule and would be coming home an hour earlier on both Tuesday and Friday nights. He hastened to assure me that his shift had nothing whatsoever to do with my foolish caper. However it came about, I am delighted with the result. We can now invite friends over for dinner on these evenings, or go to the gym and exercise together and still have some time left for one another before sleep.

The other event involved a chance visit to a co-housing community. Within three minutes I knew: This is what I want! Co-housing involves separate living units plus a common meeting house for people interested in creating shared community. Often there are community gardens, a few meals together each week, and other joint activities. It is a good solution for extroverts married to introverts or for workaholics married to folks who want a homey home. Previously unenthusiastic, Nate now seems open to the possibility of co-housing.

I marvel now at how my ideas about marriage and "happily ever after" have changed over the years. When I was younger, I thought "grown-up" was a destination. I didn't realize it would be an ongoing process of discovery, of daring to reveal more and more about who we really are. When I got married, I had no idea that our marriage contract would need to be negotiated and renegotiated in order for us to live happily ever after. And I certainly never imagined that in order to stay together and thrive as a couple, I might just have to move out.

THE SHOE

Ronnie Caplane

"TODAY WAS A GOOD DAY," I tell Wendy over dinner. "I accomplished something."

When my husband died, my full-speed-ahead lifestyle came to a screeching halt. For days, probably even weeks, I sat on the couch, traumatized, staring into space while friends scurried around setting out food, doing dishes, sorting through stacks of mail. Getting out of bed and deciding what shirt to wear with my blue jeans was all I could manage. Although I've returned to some activities, it's more form than substance. Even now, months after the fact, grieving and healing, thinking about the future and trying to figure out who I am, saps all my energy.

But today I actually did something for someone else and was feeling pretty darn good about it.

"I owe it all to Marsha," I say.

"Tell me about it," asks Wendy, falling into the rhetoric of her prior career as a therapist.

"I mailed a shoe," I announce proudly.

That morning Marsha called in a panic. She's in Washington, DC for her daughter's college graduation.

"I need you to do something for me," she said, uttering words I hadn't heard since my prior life came crashing down.

"Anything," I said.

"I need you to overnight a shoe to me," Marsha said, explaining that she had brought a mismatched pair for her daughter Beth and launching into detailed instructions involving bedrooms, shoes, and addresses.

"Wait, wait, wait," I said. "I can't empty the dishwasher and talk on the phone at the same time anymore. You're telling too much." I couldn't even remember which room was Beth's and I didn't want to mess this up. This wasn't just about a shoe. It was about Beth's graduation and Marsha's image as the all-powerful mother who could make a shoe materialize in a hotel room across the country. This was about me doing something for a friend after months of friends taking care of me. "I'll go to your house right now and call you from there. Then you can tell me what to do next."

I dashed into Marsha's house and ran upstairs cell phone in hand with Marsha's phone number preset. I figured out which room was Beth's. It had two mismatched shoes on the floor and a plaque on the door that said "Beth's Room."

I hit "send."

"I'm in," I reported when Marsha answered.

She described the shoe she needed. I studied the shoes on the floor, picked one up, and clutched it to my breast.

"Maybe I should send both." I said, suddenly worried that I had the wrong shoe. "Wouldn't two pairs be better than one? What if I have the wrong shoe?"

"You don't," she said. "Just send the one." She directed me to paper and pen, gave me the address, told me where to take the shoe and how it should be packaged.

I passed her instructions on to the woman at the UPS store in Montclair.

"This shoe has to arrive intact," I said, cradling it in my hands with a delicacy worthy of Cinderella's glass slipper. To drive home the importance of this mission, I added, "My friend's daughter needs it for her graduation on Thursday."

She took the shoe and examined it. "This is a nice shoe," she said, "but don't they sell shoes in Washington?"

Why hadn't that occurred to me?

Had Marsha engineered this crisis solely for my benefit?

"Of course they do," I said, quickly concocting what must be Marsha's rationale for mailing a shoe rather than buying new ones. "They don't have time to shop. They've got a lot of packing to do, and it's cheaper to overnight one shoe than to buy a new pair. Besides, these are good-luck shoes." I made up the last little tidbit for effect.

When I finish telling Wendy the story, I'm breathless with the enthusiasm of an important mission accomplished.

"Tomorrow by this time, the shoe will be there," I say proudly.

Wendy smiles and tells me how well I'm doing. In her smile I can see a memory of the woman who used to be me, the one for whom mailing a shoe would have been a throwaway task, something sandwiched into an already overbooked schedule. Someday maybe that woman will be back. But first I have to rebuild my life, one shoe at a time.

4

OUR CHILDREN
MOVE THROUGH US

A REGULAR GUY

Laura Shumaker

"DO YOU WANT ME to come in with you while you get your hair cut?"

"No," replies my 19-year-old son Matthew. "I want him to think I drove here by myself."

When I suggest that he remove the junior sheriff sticker from his T-shirt before he goes in, he refuses.

"I want him to think I take care of bad guys."

Matthew is autistic, and wants to be a regular guy in the worst way. But he is crippled by social awkwardness that, try as we have, we can't train out of him. Earlier in the day, we had been to the dentist, where Matthew read *The Care Bears Go to the Dentist* while waiting for his turn. To look at his face, you would think he was reading *Paradise Lost*. I sat next to him with a straight face while the packed waiting room stifled laughter. And who could blame anyone?

Most of the people in the waiting room have seen Matthew around town and wondered about him. They have seen him at the skateboard store, pretending he works there, and at the hardware store with his large hands wrapped around a bottle of weed killer, studying the label earnestly. They have seen him pushing a gas-powered lawnmower around town with a weed whacker and a leaf blower stacked on top.

What is with that kid?

Matthew doesn't want just to be a regular guy. He wants to be *the* guy, the poisonous plant and weed expert, and the lawn-care authority of our East Bay community of Lafayette. He's been known to approach strangers with warnings about deadly nightshade, oleander, and water hemlock. Some snicker and walk away, others show a glimpse of understanding and stop to chat. They make his day, and I know my smile of gratitude makes theirs.

"He would be really good-looking if he weren't autistic," my 12-year-old son says of Matthew, and as unkind as it sounds, I know what he means. Matthew is very handsome, with a tall and wiry frame, broad shoulders, and sandy blond hair. His eyebrows arch dramatically to frame his brown eyes, and his jaw is square and masculine. But his exaggerated expressions and body carriage set him apart from the regular guys he would like to identify with. His forehead twists with intensity, he smiles too suddenly and too widely, his hungry-for-friendship gaze is desperate. He doesn't pick up on subtle social cues, like when to step back, when to change the subject from poisonous plants to *anything* more universal, and he doesn't understand that it is not cool to ask a girl if she has ever had a seizure. He likes to wear dark socks and sandals, shorts, and a T-shirt that says "Shumaker Landscaping," with our phone number below. The phone number, of course, is not for soliciting business as Matthew would like to believe, but for identification purposes.

"Is this Shumaker Landscaping? There is a man mowing my lawn, and I already have a gardener. Could you please get him to stop?"

Matthew has been attending Camphill Special School in Pennsylvania since he was 16, the year he decided that he should drive a car like a regular guy and drove my car through a wall in our garage. There were other close calls. One day during his freshman year at our local high school, he observed a guy pushing his girlfriend flirtatiously and then tapping her on the head. When Matthew tried the same move with too much force, I was summoned to his school where he was crying in the principal's office. "Joe did it to Sue, and she liked it!" Just when we thought things were calming down following this incident at school, we got a letter from an attorney asking us to contact him about a bicycle accident involving Matthew. It turned out that while riding his bike the month before, Matthew had apparently collided with a young boy on his bike.

"Matthew? What's this about a bike accident?"

"Who told you?"

"Someone sent me a letter. Was the boy you bumped into hurt?"

"Pretty much."

Dear God.

"Was he bleeding?"

"Probably. Am I in trouble?"

My husband and I came to the heartbreaking conclusion that Matthew was no longer safe in the community where he had grown up, and his impulsive actions were putting others in peril. He needed more supervision, more than we or the local school could provide.

But the good news now is that Matthew is thriving at Camphill, and is an important part of its community of disabled people. He goes to class, cooks, and does his own laundry. He prunes trees, tends an organic garden, and takes care of the grass. During the winter he shovels snow gleefully, and has become fascinated with weather patterns in the Northeast. He brags about his newfound responsibilities, and tells us he is good at hard things. When he graduates from this school, he hopes to live in the Camphill community in Santa Cruz, California.

But he'll be home for Christmas, and if you're lucky, you might spot him walking around town with his garden tools, rain or shine, just a regular working guy. His mother is the blond hiding behind the wheel of her Toyota Highlander, or behind a bush, keeping her eye on her first-born son. Just a regular mom with a giant lump in her throat.

MOTHERS IN ARMS

Janis Mitchell

MOMS TALK EASILY to each other, and sometimes we open up some pretty deep places to people we don't even know. I was at a school concert this morning sitting beside a woman I had never met before. I asked her if she had a performer in the show, and she told me that her son was to be singing with the fifth-graders. There was something in her tone that made me ask her if he was her only child. She smiled with contentment and said, "He's it. He's my guy." Then she asked me about my child. I told her I had a new freshman singing in the program: my one and only. Because of something I saw in her face I added, "Eleven years in the making." She nodded and said simply, "Eight." We sat companionably together, and I thought about the understanding among women who have fought in the Infertility Wars.

When I was 19 years old I developed uterine blood clots from birth control pills. I remember saying a little prayer that I would be compatible with a new birth control device prescribed by our family doctor. It was called the Dalkon Shield. Intrauterine devices were very popular among young women in the early '70s, and they caused infertility in a generation of us. We didn't know until our mid-twenties, or later, that we had sustained such terrible damage. One friend miscarried in the first trimester so many times that she gave up trying to carry a pregnancy to term. Others, like me, suffered infections that left us with scarring and endometriosis, blocked or blown-out fallopian tubes. It was only through intervention by infertility specialists (bless them for doing this work) that we were able to conceive at all. My daughter is the product of In Vitro Fertilization, and I know many others like her and many mothers who endured everything medical science had to offer so they could have these children.

We were the fortunate ones. I know women who did their research and simply couldn't face the ordeal of infertility treatment. Some women friends have tried In Vitro repeatedly and given up when it no longer made medical or financial sense to continue. Some became parents through adoption, and others for whatever reason weren't able to take this step and had to accept that they would never be mothers at all. One friend persisted until she learned that her husband was contributing abundant, motile (actively moving), but unable-to-penetrate block-headed sperm. As my daughter would say, "How random is that?"

When I did become a mother I gloried in my new role. I capped off the reservoir of emotional pain and opened my heart to fully experience what many women take for granted. I was thrilled to participate in any "mommy and me"–style activity. I took my daughter to preschool music class and Gymboree every week. I made contact with other new moms on walks and outings in the park. I had been welcomed into the ultimate sisterhood. Age, race, class, educational background, religion: none of these separated us when we talked about motherhood. New moms are a source of vital support to one another—even on the difficult days. I am remembering the day my friend Elizabeth had handled a screaming baby for hours and then at five o'clock called her husband at work and said, "Derek, I'm on my first beer. . . ." She shared that story with me, and I howled with laughter; at times, I had felt like doing exactly the same thing.

After a year or two the other moms began to plan for their second child. I watched as every one of my friends who wanted to became pregnant and had a new baby. Two more IVF attempts failed, and I acknowledged that our daughter was to be our only child. Even though I was already a mom, it hurt. I recall running into an acquaintance from Gymboree one day as she was showing off her second one and saying something to her about having tried to have another. She cut me off with "I already know your story," as if hearing it again would direct the attention away from her joy and toward my sorrow. Not to worry, a beautiful new baby trumps just about any subject. I know the hurt I felt wasn't only from being shut out of the two-time mommy club. It wasn't even limited to thwarted maternal desire. It was exactly like my friend Anne said 15 years after her only child was born: "I look around and I think, where are my other children?" I have wondered this myself.

Even though I know how fortunate I am to have my daughter, I sometimes imagine what it would have been like to have mothered a different sort of child. This might be someone whose genetic mix would have blended other parts of my husband and me, a boy instead of a girl or a person who resembles me just a little bit. I'm sure my daughter would have benefited from having a sibling. As it is, summer camp and, one day, a college dormitory are the closest she will come to knowing what it is like to share her bedroom and live closely with others. She has never had to share her parents. We have tried not to load her up with the responsibility of being The Child upon whom all hopes and dreams and bragging rights rest. I do not want her to feel that kind of pressure.

I have always clearly known that the tenacious pursuit of parenthood over 11 years of medical intervention was my choice and have tried not to link it in any way to my daughter's life. I did not go through this for *her*; I did it for me. It was a time in my life when I was empowered to fight the odds and win not by virtue of any talent or skill but by pure stubbornness, strength of will, and simple good luck. I share a deep knowledge with other mothers who are veterans of the Infertility Wars. When we sit in the audience listening to our children sing, we know that we almost didn't make it, and we are just so happy to be here.

SENIOR MOMMY

Karen L. Pliskin

WHEN MY GRANDMOTHER was my age, she had a seven-year-old granddaughter—me. When my mother was my age, she had a daughter who was a graduate student in anthropology—also me. At 57, they were middle-aged housewives with empty nests. I, on the other hand, am the 57-year-old mother of a seventh-grader.

The same week that my daughter entered kindergarten, I was invited to join official seniordom with a startling invitation from the AARP that snuggled in the mail among my birthday cards. I threw the envelope in the garbage can and dumped coffee grounds on top of it so my husband wouldn't see that the world outside our house knew I was 50. How could I possibly be a senior, when just five years earlier I had given birth?

When our daughter started kindergarten, I looked around at the other mothers. A few looked 50 too, but I didn't ask. Sun worship could have aged their skin prematurely. No one, including me, had gray hair. Most looked to be in their thirties. I was probably the oldest mom in the school, but no one had to know. No one talked about age directly, and I certainly wasn't going to give away any information that could hint that I was in college in the late '60s.

As a midlife mother of a middle-schooler, I am out of sync with the age-appropriate role my culture expects me to perform. And as an anthropologist, I can't help but observe that American culture presumes 50-year-olds will contemplate retirement, have children in college or earning their own living, and become grandparents. In fact, a study conducted by the National Center for Health Statistics in 2000 found that the average age of first-time grandmothers in the United States was 47. Not only are women over 50 depicted as grandmothers, they are also seen as postmenopausal beings who regard sex as a thing of the past. Even medical research on sexually transmitted diseases surveys women in the reproductive 18- to 44-year category, with the

underlying assumption that women over 44 are not getting sexually transmitted diseases because they are not sexually active.

In reality, the incidence of older women becoming mothers is
increasing in the U.S., as the Center for Health Statistics reported
in 2003. The birthrate for women in the 40-to-44 age category
doubled since 1981, and topped 100,000 in 2003, while the birthrate for women between 45 and 54 years of age increased by 0.5%.

I only wish our culture would catch up with the social and
biological realities of moms like me. Instead, retirement commu-
nities advertise for residents aged 50 and over. Exercise classes for
seniors aim for 50 on up. Some stores start their senior discounts
at age 55. These cultural representations of seniordom pervade
television and magazine articles as well as advertising images.
And they don't apply to me.

But as the mother of a kindergartner, I was embarrassed by my
age. I kept telling Eliana, our daughter, not to tell anyone how
old I was. She was quite good about concealing my secret,
although she couldn't figure out why I didn't want anyone to
know, since age is a curiosity of children and a characteristic by
which they compare others to themselves.

"Mommy?" she asked one day when I picked her up from her
first-grade class. "Do you know that Ashley's mom is 28, and her
grandma is 50?"

I knew it was coming. Someone *would* have a grandmother
younger than I.

"Well, sweetie," I answered, "when I was 28, I was in grad
school and planning on going to Iran for my doctoral studies."

"Why did you wait so long to marry Daddy?"

"I didn't meet Daddy until I was 39, and we didn't get married
until I was 43. Anyway, I was having a good time traveling and
doing research, and you might want to do that too."

If my daughter imitates my behavioral history, I'll be a 90-
year-old first-time grandmother—hopefully not wheelchair-
bound in a convalescent home or too feeble to hold an infant.

My age was Eliana's and my little secret until the second half
of first grade, when the children wrote short stories about their
parents. These were posted on the teacher's bulletin board in the

hallway. To my horror, there it was, spelling having been corrected by the teacher:

"My Mommy is 51. My Daddy is 42. My Daddy is a physicist. He works at LBL. My Mommy is an artist and an anthropologist."

I wanted to sink into the floor. If I were aghast at everyone knowing my age, I could only imagine the discomfort that the lesbian moms of one of my daughter's classmates must have felt when they read their child's description of fights, separation, and wishes that her moms would live together again. We parents were reading each child's family description, finding out private information that could form the basis of a juvenile Jerry Springer show. I then knew the ages of every parent whose child was in Eliana's class, and was mostly surprised that those I thought were close to my age were not. I was, by far, the oldest mom. I longed to strangle the teacher for her audacity in publicizing what some parents might consider very private information.

More than six years have passed since that disconcerting incident, and I am already nostalgic for Eliana's early school years. Now in middle school, she is growing up and entering the self-consciousness of adolescence. But I, too, am growing up. Having found and befriended several other mothers in their fifties when Eliana was in elementary school spurred me—and them—to be proud older moms.

No longer embarrassed about being one of the oldest mothers in my daughter's school, I happily tell my years if asked. In fact, when I look around me, I have no idea whether women I see are in their late thirties, forties, or fifties. Among ourselves, we older moms joke about our anomalous status, and enjoy the expressions on the faces of younger parents when they find out our ages. We are energetic, vibrant, fun-loving, sexual women. Grandparenting is far from our minds. We have too much to do.

As a woman of 57, I undoubtedly don't fit into society's expectations of my age. After taking off years from work to be a mother half-time and an artist half-time, I still think I have a career ahead of me, like many younger stay-at-home moms. I am not looking forward to retirement. Physically, I am more active now than I ever was in my youth. I learned to cross-country ski six years ago, and when my daughter started ice-skating classes at the age of seven, I began figure skating lessons at the age of 52.

In fact, I can't imagine having spent my twenties and thirties in the throes of parenting. During those years I studied and traveled to third-world countries, stayed in sleazy no-star hotels, and experienced remote cultures that enriched me as a person. I doubt that empty-nesters who became parents when I was wandering the world would attempt the kind of adventurous travel in middle age that I encountered years ago. Even for me now, a simple two-star hotel won't do.

Sometimes, though, I wonder whether Eliana is comfortable with my age.

"Guess what happened at the movies last night!" I proclaimed to her recently. "I got a discount ticket because I'm 57 and they think I'm a senior. And Daddy had to pay full price."

"That's funny." Her eyes sparkled. She was grinning.

"Hey!" I grabbed her, and we polka-ed around the kitchen humming "The Lonely Goatherd" from *The Sound of Music*. "Are you embarrassed that I'm one of the oldest moms you know?"

"No, why? Lucy's mom's 54. And so is Jakie's mom. And Alex's mom is 56. Rebecca's mom's 56, too."

I smiled. My generation has elasticized the age of motherhood. I just hope that by the time my daughter becomes an adult, cultural images of middle-aged mothers with their young children will be common—and depictions of seniorhood will start at age 70.

THE PUJA

Diana Divecha

THE DAY BEFORE my 13-year-old daughter's Hindu coming-of-age ceremony, I am field commander of a small army. I stand on my Berkeley deck overlooking our backyard, a cell phone in one pocket and a notebook of lists in the other. The yard below swarms with my Indian men (husband, uncles, friends) and my tall blond Minnesotan nephews. They are setting up a microphone, speakers, and 150 chairs in our backyard.

"Diana, love, do you know where the fishing line is? We're ready to hang the canopy," my Australian friend shouts up to me.

"In the top drawer in the family room off the lower deck!"

Miraculously, I know everything. My mind is a control room, and I am monitoring several screens simultaneously: The ladies over 70 are at the guest cottage in the backyard stringing flowers for my daughter's garland and to decorate doorways. The men over 70 are touring the grounds, examining recent home improvements. Aloo parathas and freshly sprouted mung salad are on the table, ready for lunch. My 16-year-old daughter Zai is touring her cousins around San Francisco. My mother is out shopping for a dupatta; the long Indian scarf will be just the right flourish for her pantsuit. Mia, the 13-year-old epicenter of all this action, organizes a bowl of nine different lentils for the ceremony to the nine planets. I reach for my cell phone to call the photographer—I want him to record this beehive of activity, not just for its aesthetics but for the journey it represents. The doorbell rings. The 16 bags of rose petals have arrived.

Twenty-two years ago I was hard-pressed to find Bombay on a map, yet I married my graduate school love, Arjun, who was from that city. Mixed-race marriage had been legal for about 20 years, but in my small hometown in northern Minnesota, it was still unheard of. "Can they do that?" my grandfather asked my mother, and indeed, my childhood Lutheran church refused to marry us. My family fretted: perhaps I'd be shipped off to India, perhaps my future half-and-half children would grow up confused, and what about those mistresses Indian men have? My fellow doctoral candidate friends in New York worried aloud that Indian men might be sexually strange, and articles about Indian bride-burning mysteriously appeared on my desk. When I arrived in Bombay for our Indian wedding, the air was rife with just as many concerns: there was astonishment among Arjun's urban social circles that I was from a "village," and dismay at my six-foot height, "skimpy" hair, and pink skin, and of course fear of the high American divorce rate.

Since my own family could not make the trip to India, I was swept along with no one to turn to for support. The day before my wedding, my hands were painted in the traditional henna mendhi, and future in-laws sang insulting songs about me and my family whom they'd never met—a ritualized venting against the in-laws cloaked in humor. It was not the last time I'd feel I was in someone else's play without knowing my lines. The next day, wrapped in a sari and jewels and flowers, I was married in a Hindu ceremony in which Arjun and I unconventionally took turns leading the walk around the marriage fire, and I promised to feed and care for anyone who would visit my home.

Arjun and I settled in Berkeley, so I made it my business to learn about my husband's culture and family. In many ways it was easy: the aesthetics, the sensibilities, the spirituality and ancient wisdom and civilization of India were all attractive. But as an anthropologist friend advised, it is for good reason that some cultures have in-law taboos. Indeed, threading understanding and acceptance across the in-law divide posed our greatest challenge. Little acts and small conversations took on great symbolism. Turf battles ensued with my Indian extended family over rearranging the refrigerator and feeding the children as we sorted out the traditional top-down direction of power in the family.

My Scandinavian family redefined a "real man" as they tried to find common ground with a foreign man who didn't hunt, fish, or even eat meat, but was instead into technology and books. We all engaged in an artful, ongoing dance of limits and boundaries on the one hand, and persistent generosity and forgiveness on the other. A faith in good intentions helped soothe the sting of misunderstandings. Ultimately Arjun and I believed that as our own loving relationship thrived, and our girls grew into a comfortable bicultural life, our families would follow suit.

Two decades and two daughters after beginning this journey, I am preparing to feed and care for 150 guests to our home, 37 of whom are extended family members from both sides. My mother-in-law Malu had attended the small family coming-of-age puja we'd had for our older daughter, and now she wants to make sure that no one from her family misses this second puja. "This may be it for me," she admits. "I may not be here for the girls' weddings." Though at 75 she is healthy as an ox, I acquiesce and prepare for a wave of guests. A small part of me feels drawn to the edge of the unknown, and I have a flicker of intuition that perhaps there is some larger agenda, a godly script unfolding here.

In the middle of preparing gifts, maps, itineraries, cars, and accommodations for the out-of-towners, Mia is my second-in-command, a real organizer. We spend hours in the car, running errands and talking. We talk about being graceful in the center of attention and the importance of our guests' presence, and we talk about the heart of the ceremony. Of all of us, Mia is perhaps the most spiritual and the most knowledgeable about Hindu practice. Every morning she sits in front of her bedroom altar and brings her spirit into focus, with a chant in Hindi, a brief prayer and meditation, and of course the tasty prasad (the sweets, nuts, or dried fruit offered to the gods), which our dog waits for silently by her side. To Mia, the puja is a natural extension and an honoring of that which she has already been cultivating. To me, the ritual is a pause to celebrate 13-year-old Mia as much as it is a moment to honor our family work of keeping both cultures open to our daughters.

The morning of the ceremony dawns cold and foggy. Friends and relatives come early to help. The first person in the gray morning light is our friend, the girls' godmother Elnora, who bends over a sack of flowers on my front deck. Like the shrouded early-morning street dwellers in India, she works silently in the dawn, arranging purple, pink, and yellow aster heads into colorful mandalas down our walkways. Soon the food starts to arrive.

Aunties clip lemongrass and grate ginger for the gallons of chai tea simmering on the stove.

I check on Mia. Her room is a buzz of feminine fussing, Technicolor-saried women checking jewelry, pinning clothes, tucking flowers into hair. Mia is dressed in a traditional chanya choli: a pink and gold brocade blouse and floor-length green and yellow skirt, with gold jewelry at her neck, ears, and wrists. Her hands, painted in the same deep-red lacy mendhi that I wore at my wedding, are relaxed and folded in her lap. Her dark eyes shine with excitement, and I slipstream in her joy. I kiss her on the forehead, we privately exchange endearments, and I return her to the good hands that are guiding her.

I walk outside to the transformed garden, my arms loaded with shawls for shivering friends. The lawn and decks are filling with guests. To many, we are sharing our Hinduism for the first time, and I suddenly view the event through the eyes of my relatives who have never been to India. The scene is deeply colorful in pinks, reds, and oranges against the green of the garden, and there are flowers, mandalas, gods and goddesses everywhere. Sitar and tabla music float down from the musicians perched on the hill. Will this ever make sense to my relatives, this synthesis of two cultures that I love? Suddenly I'm flooded with doubt, as the distance between where I began and where I am now is suddenly laid bare. My brother steps forward and hugs me, and my forest of giant Scandinavian nephews looms quietly nearby.

"Have I already hugged you?" my 20-year-old nephew twinkles. "Doesn't matter, I'll do it again." I exhale, and am deeply ready.

The inner circle of family gathers in the middle of the yard, on the rug next to the officiating pandit, Mrs. Duneja. Banks of Mia's friends sit just behind her, and extended family and friends sit on rugs or chairs on the lawn, fanning out from our circle. Mia takes the microphone first, welcoming one and all, naming honored guests and those who have come from afar. "And I want to acknowledge those who can't be with us," she continues, "especially Bhagwan, Papa's Papa, who died 25 years ago." Tears make eyes sparkle, intimacy deepens instantly, and the tone is set.

Next, I introduce the puja's meaning for us, and how we

bridge Eastern philosophy and Western psychology in our family. A developmental psychologist, I describe the enormous changes that occur in 13-year-olds, creating both vulnerabilities and opportunities. "These changes make for a sensitive moment in which to bring together Mia's community of friends, relatives, and teachers to help support her on this path that she's begun to travel." Finally, I introduce our pandit, and the ceremony begins.

Mrs. Duneja is a tiny woman with a huge stature. She emanates a calm, relaxed, informal demeanor, helping us to feel comfortable. She pins the microphone to her shawl and begins. "The basic message of the Hindu holy books is to live in peace and harmony with our own inner self, with other people, and with nature."

As Pandit Duneja pauses to offer a Sanskrit prayer, the clouds part and sunlight streams into the yard, bathing Mia in a golden light. An energy breathes through the group, and Mia beams. Mrs. Duneja turns to talk to Mia directly and guides her to a way of life that is aspirational, achievement-oriented, and generous. Then, to the rhythm of Mrs. Duneja's chant, we offer a mix of lentils and rice and flowers to the fire, the representation of god. Afterwards, she offers Mia a box in which to collect money for the poor, and a gold necklace in which she has written the Gayatri Mantra, a super-mantra that all Hindus know. We pray, chant, and meditate. Even my father, who finds his god in the forest, holds his hands together in prayer in the Hindu way. Mia comes to take blessings from her family. Rose petals float through the air for minutes, and Mia receives them with a wide smile and open arms.

Arjun invites the guests to lunch on the decks where our Indian aunts, uncles, and cousins serve lunch and explain each of the Indian dishes—samosas, bhel puri, dosas, sambar, and dohklas. For many of my family members, it is their first time eating this foreign food—snacks that would be enjoyed on street corners in Bombay. And they are delighting in it. As the music drifts out over the yard, people mix easily and a joyful sense of fulfillment settles over the space. Mia's teachers take their lunch out near the big Ganesh next to the creek, and they are soon joined by

Arjun's cousins to share stories. An American friend finds Arjun's cousin to discuss yoga and meditation. I introduce some of my favorite women to my dad, describing their special gifts and accomplishments to him.

"Well, I have a story," my usually quiet dad replies. Surprised, we are attentive. He begins to tell the story of meeting Arjun for the first time, how I brought this lonely Indian guy home for Christmas. "We knew there was something to this relationship, even though they weren't letting on," he went on, nodding toward me. "Arjun's such a super guy. He's taught our family so much. He's changed our family."

A mixed group of men gather with chai in hand and begin to tell jokes. The laughter is contagious, and pretty soon addresses and invitations to visit one another's homes are shared. Mia and her friends snake among the guests handing out gifts of bangles, silver coins, and prasad, the sweets that were blessed during the ceremony. Inevitably teenagers from both sides of the family find each other and begin to mingle, as young people always do at such events. Something new is taking hold, growing. My mother-in-law walks over to me and slips her arm around my waist. My arm goes easily over her shoulders. "All that hard work paid off, didn't it?" she smiles at me. I return her smile, acknowledging in a moment both the work of the puja preparations and the knitting together of families. She pats my arm affectionately and moves on.

Days after the tamasha festivity is over, the puja area remains undisturbed in the yard. The rose petals strewn about begin to curl, and the altar gathers the morning dew. I visit it often, sitting quietly, renewing myself in this powerful space. As the energy of my garden feels permanently changed, so, too, Mia's future, and at last, the course of our two families.

KEEPING FAITH AND LETTING GO

Karen Mulvaney

RAISING CHILDREN is a constant lesson in faith and letting go, as I learned well one season during a time my son was running cross-country on a high school team. Before my husband Tom and I even knew he had any interest in running, Mason, a freshman, had joined the cross-country team and started training. As the fall progressed, I picked him up after practice, which was held at school every day. Arriving around 5:30, I met him in the parking lot as he finished the daily run. To my amazement, a few weeks into the season, Mason arrived at my car, red-faced and panting, with news that he had just completed a 13-mile run. It was clear that he had a natural talent for running and was becoming quite good at the sport.

When Tom and I watched him compete, we were struck by the physical toll of cross-country. Our son and his teammates would expend such vast amounts of physical effort that frequently after a competition their legs would buckle, sending them sprawling on the grass, and many would become sick to their stomachs. They endured excruciating muscle pain and body cramps as they pushed through their discomfort. Many decided this sport was not for them or because of chronic injuries could not compete.

On race days, we would rise with the sun to get ready and be treated to a vivid sky filled with blazing color. As we waited for the events to begin, we listened to the sweet quiet of the morning and the unfolding of a new day. The natural surroundings where meets were held, the beauty of the early morning, the rolling green hills, and root-strewn dirt trails, all combined in such a way to be a spiritual experience for me. Watching these emerging young men and women go through this mental and physical test was a tribute to their spirit and perseverance. Their belief in themselves and their willingness to commit to such a sport was inspiring. The team would often chide other sports teams by saying that cross-country was the only completely pure sport, because there was no ball, no racquet, no court, no excuses, just the runner, his shoes, and the earth beneath him, covering the distance, step by step, mile after mile.

As Mason entered his sophomore year, he continued to run, but his body was changing, working against him. He had gone from being a tall, super-lean freshman to a larger version of himself, filled out, with bigger muscles, increased height, and more body weight. It was during this season that we were given an opportunity to watch him also grow in independence, and we learned a good lesson ourselves in letting go as parents.

Mason was scheduled to run an important race and had substantial pressure on him to perform. Tom felt the pressure, too. He had traveled extensively during Mason's childhood, missing a great deal of time with our son. When he was able to be home, his emotions were heightened watching Mason compete. We both had participated in sports during our own high school years. Now, when we watched our children, we found our emotional memories stirred up.

The night before the meet, one of only four school dances that year was scheduled; it would be over later than was optimal for racing the next day. Mason wanted to participate in social events at school and had decided he was definitely going to this dance. He could stay out late and race the next day, he said, and it wouldn't change how he ran. We urged him to come home early and get rest, but we also realized that Mason would have to make this decision on his own. He felt quite able to do both well and made the decision to go to the dance and come home when it was over. We stood back and let him be.

The next day, as we got up to get ready for the race, Tom was irritated and said he could not watch Mason that day. He was too nervous and invested in the outcome, the possibility that Mason would not do well. I urged Tom to come to the competition, hoping we could stand firm with Mason. I felt we owed him support for making his own decisions. I wanted us to be able to witness Mason's race, success or not. Tom relented and said he would come, but the decision was difficult.

As we drove to the race, a good 30 minutes away, I could feel the tension, as if it took up a whole seat in the car. The day was brilliant, though, and we began to enjoy the outdoors, as we always did on race days. We urged each other to let go of our worries, the need to have Mason do well, and just be there for him.

Finally, the event he was scheduled to run was called. We could not even stand together to watch. Tom went one direction, and I went another as we strained to get a good view of the runners, searching for the familiar shape of our son. Minutes ticked by as we watched and hoped, and finally we could see him. He was up in the front pack, keeping pace with the fastest group. It felt as if Tom and I were running in the race too, trying to catch every glimpse of the pack of runners, over and around the bend, up and down each hill and valley.

The race was close to finishing, and as the runners made the final loop around the course, Mason moved well in front. As he completed the last part of the race, headed for first place, Tom and I looked at each other across the vast expanse of green grass, our hearts full of joy. Mason had won the race, set a meet record, and done it on his own terms. We stood in the field, the sun bright. Mason basked in the victory he earned. But Tom and I were elated, too. By having faith in our son, win or lose, we also had been rewarded.

THE ENCHANTED CASTLE CAKE

Risa Nye

IT'S BEEN 18 YEARS since I spent an evening awkwardly curled up on the couch, sniffling through a movie based on Virginia Woolf's *To the Lighthouse*. Pregnant with my third child, my heart was captured by six-year-old James, a blond charmer in a sailor suit. The last of six children, James Ramsay had a special place in his mother's heart: he was "the most gifted and sensitive of her children." James wanted desperately to go to the lighthouse, enticingly visible yet painfully distant from the Ramsays' summer home—a daylong trip that would have been a very big adventure for such a small boy. In the story, young James does not get to the lighthouse; not until he is a surly 16-year-old and far beyond his childhood longing does the day finally arrive. I'm not sure why I reacted to the movie with such strong sentiment, barely able to stop the flood of tears—maybe it was hormones, or maybe it was that I knew I was carrying a boy, my last child, just like Mrs. Ramsay's James, and watching the unraveling of his innocence was almost more than I could bear.

We named our son James, partly after Woolf's moving story. He was born blond, like James Ramsay, and had big blue questioning eyes. My James was a quiet observer. We would catch him staring intently at the white-on-white chevron pattern of our couch. It was a bit odd, but we put his little infant seat near the couch so he could stare to his heart's content. As he got older, James was fascinated with many things, especially letters and words. He read his birthday cards out loud at his fourth birthday party. He has always been happy around books and, like me, rarely goes anywhere without something to read.

When James was small, we had a few children's cookbooks. Every now and again we would do a baking or a cooking project together—snickerdoodles were a big hit with all three kids. At a garage sale, I found a true classic: *Betty Crocker's Cookbook for Boys and Girls*, written circa 1957. It was fun to read and to look at—the drawings were priceless, and the recipes harked back to my childhood favorites, especially cinnamon toast, pigs in blankets, jam-filled thumbprint cookies, and macaroni and cheese.

But James was entranced by the Enchanted Castle Cake. It was more than just a cake; it was an architectural marvel. The castle was constructed by cleverly sawing a 9x13-inch cake (yellow, from a mix) into smaller squares, rectangles, and arches, then artfully stacking and arranging the pieces, applying frosting (also from a mix), and decorating the whole affair with marshmallows, chocolate, inverted ice cream cones, and toothpicks to create an impressive castle with flags, turrets, and a drawbridge. James really, really wanted to make that castle cake, but there was always something more pressing to do. Promises were made to make it someday, but that day never came.

In October 1991, when James was five, our house burned to the ground in the Oakland hills fire. Although my husband thought to rescue our big binder of handwritten recipes, the *Cookbook for Boys and Girls* was lost, along with everything else. I don't think I understood how much this book was missed until James started talking about the castle cake again. How would I ever find a copy of this book, long out of print? As it turned out, a neighbor whose house didn't burn made it her job to help the rest of us replace our favorite cookbooks. To those of us starting all over, having our favorite recipes again allowed us to start putting our lives back together. In an unfamiliar rental house, an unfamiliar neighborhood, and a different kitchen, being able to cook family favorites was a blessing.

I gave up trying to replace my vintage Betty Crocker, but then Paula, the neighbor with foodie connections, put me in touch with a man from General Mills, Betty Crocker's parent company. We talked about the *Cookbook for Boys and Girls*, and I explained my five-year-old son's fascination with the Enchanted Castle Cake. Oh yes, he was familiar with the castle cake. Yes, he had a copy of the cookbook. No, I couldn't have it. But he offered to copy the recipe and illustrations and send it to me, which he did, and hope was restored in James's heart. I confess I did not jump right up and bake the cake. It was still a huge hassle, and besides,

I didn't have anything to bake with yet. In fact, it was nearly a year after the fire before I felt like baking anything.

There is a happy ending to our story, however. One summer day, when James was 12, we made the castle cake. Our cake had a definite starboard list to it, and I doubt the turrets would have survived even a minor earthquake. We took some license and liberally doused the whole structure with multicolored sprinkles—it was a party castle. We did all of it together—placing the marshmallows like puffy luminaria atop the castle walls, frosting the upside-down ice cream cones, creating waves of blue icing (for the moat, of course), placing jaunty little paper flags into the tops of the tilted towers—the whole shebang. Our special touch: chocolate dorsal fins placed menacingly in the moat. I took several pictures, for it was a sight to behold. If, after all those years, it didn't meet his expectations, James never let on.

James graduated from high school in June 2004, and we packed him off to college. Although he is no longer that dreamy, bookish five-year-old—or the not-yet-teen who could still have fun baking with his mom—we will always share the sweet memory of the day we made the Enchanted Castle Cake.

CHINESE EASTER
True Fortunes from Chef Chao's

Dorothy Moore

EASTER SUNDAY because I had to work we went for Chinese food.
Something special. Usually we hunt eggs with cousins,
a long walk after dinner with Grandpa.

These are my children, my husband, my fortunes, my love:

Fragile 11 Alec. Humorous gentleman, his father's echo: be careful
Mom, we don't want to spend all our money, guiding my new car
purchase.

The constructive use of riches is better than their possession.

Julia, lily of the valley. Even-keeled 12 on the precipice.
Corrects my parking. Her notebook entwined with
flowers and hearts.
So *blond*, her older brother says.

Carve your name on heart and not on marble.

Prodigal not quite home at 17, Duncan. Sinking report card,
blooming social life. (Over my dead body you're getting a tattoo.)
Let him be who he is.
Zip your lips mom and he's right.

Trust your intuition. The universe is guiding your life.

My husband, Jeff. Honest. Guileless. Hard work his only vice.
He always asks why are you so beautiful? My little bit of heart
without the worried knots of my life.

Your kindness is surely to be repaid.

Myself. The one I cannot see. I must remember,
spinning the lazy Susan at the center of our table, there is
my sustenance; here is my food. I must remember to love.

Among the lucky, you are the chosen one.

LOVE LONG DISTANCE

Phyllis Nagle

"PETE, WHAT ARE YOU DOING?"

I looked out my bedroom window. My husband Jon had come home to watch our young sons so I could lock myself in my bedroom to cry alone about an angry client and a business deal that had fallen apart. My blond-haired, ten-year-old son was standing on a wooden chair outside my window, holding up a cardboard sign on which he had written in bold letters, "*Mom, I'm sorry the man was mean to you. I love you.*"

My second son, Pete, was always sensitive to the needs and feelings of others. His friends would call and he would give them encouragement. When a good friend of mine died, young Pete was the first to call their son to offer support.

In our small suburb outside San Francisco, I was known as "Sean's mom" or "Pete's mom" by parents who admired our sons. My sons were my best friends.

"Pete, Sean, can you two help me out—should I use this ad for my business or that other one? What do you think of . . .? Please, help me with this. . ." Pete and Sean were always there for advice.

Both went to the nearby university for college. Pete loved Berkeley and said that he would settle there after school. Sean wasn't sure where he would settle. Two years later Sean surprised us and moved to our same suburb where he had grown up. I was delighted.

After college and graduate school, Pete worked in a local law firm. One day at a football pregame party, he waved us over to chat with some of his friends.

"Mom, I want you to meet Cathy." I watched them look at one another, and thought, this may be *the one.*

After introductions, Pete glanced back at me as if to say, "Don't you think she's really cool?"

As I had predicted, several years later Jon and I found ourselves traveling to meet Cathy's parents for an engagement party in the

Pacific Northwest. Cathy had gone to college in Berkeley for four years and after graduation worked in San Francisco. I was convinced they would live in the area like Sean and his family.

The engagement party took place in Washington on a cold stormy day as we were swept into Cathy's parents' home by a strong wind. We met everyone, her parents, sisters, brothers, aunts, uncles, and grandparents. After the first hour of our visit, we learned they all lived nearby.

"May I help you in the kitchen?" I asked.

"Oh, come join us, but relax, Cathy always helps me. Besides, you're the guest. We can chat while we add a few finishing touches."

I watched as Cathy and her mom arranged the buffet items, with a sprig of this and that. The two worked in perfect unison without any conversation as if each read the other's mind. After they completed their tasks, they smiled at each other, and we all went into the next room.

After the party, on the ride home, I said, "Jon, I have this awful feeling. I think Pete and Cathy might move to Washington after the wedding."

"No way, Pete will always live in California. Don't worry."

Six months after the wedding, Pete called. "Mom," he hesitated.

I filled in the gap, "Hi, Pete. What's up?"

"Well," he stammered.

"Yes?"

"I already talked to Dad and—don't make this hard on me— I know how you feel, but Cathy and I have decided to move to Washington. We leave in four months."

I cried for days. I couldn't accept his decision to move.

One day while attending a ladies' luncheon, I overheard a tactless remark from one mother to another. "So you're complaining that your daughter has moved to New York to work and you're lonely. Seems to me you want to keep your daughter *a little girl* so that she never grows up."

Was I also being selfish to want my son nearby and not allow for his happiness? My love for him would not change; it could stretch all the way to Washington.

I decided to change my attitude. Holding back tears on their departure day, I hugged Pete and Cathy goodbye.

Several months later, we visited them in their new Craftsman house, a similar style to the one they had rented in Berkeley.

We sat down in their cozy living room. Cathy had a flair for decorating and the dark wood stood out against the warm colors of the Oriental rugs and the painting that hung above the fireplace.

"We love your home," I said.

"Well, it's not Berkeley," Pete blurted out.

Silence followed. In spite of the relaxed setting, there was tension among all of us. I could see the tightness in my son's face.

After that first visit, our trips to their home became more relaxed. The following spring we spent a sunny day in their back-yard. Pete asked Jon and me to help plant a new garden with them. We began to work as a team. On our fifth trip we met our new granddaughter. From then on, we began to look forward to our trips north.

Six years and two beautiful granddaughters later, we all have settled into our comfortable roles. The night after a recent Christmas, the living room smelled of evergreens. The tiny lights glowed on the Christmas tree. Cathy and I were in the brightly lit kitchen. She stirred the thick onion soup. Sitting next to the warmth of the fireplace, Pete and Jon watched over little Mary as she cooed in her infant seat. Our three-year-old granddaughter, Wendy, called to me from her perch on the lower step in the den.

"Grandma, can you come play with my new dollhouse?"

Cathy gave me a smile. She read my mind.

"I can manage the dinner," Cathy said. "I know you want to be with Wendy."

She was right. With great enthusiasm, I joined my grand-daughter to peek into the painted wooden house and play with the tiny dolls inside. I could see the others in the next room. Our son called out to Jon as he stoked the fire. "Dad, do you think I should put more logs on?"

We're a close family even if we are separated by many miles. The best part of having sons married is acquiring new best friends—grandchildren.

A NORMAL GRANDMA

Kathleen Faraday

WHEN I WAS MOVING my mother into her new assisted-living facility, I came across one of my school papers that she had saved. It was titled "My Road to Somewhere." I thought about who I was at the time with the whole world stretched out before me. I wondered how it would have read if I'd written it today. Would it be that different? Perhaps not.

I often say that I'm not certain what I want to be when I grow up. And how did I get to be a grandma? I couldn't possibly be that old. As we go about placing one foot in front of the other, following the paths that appear to be exciting or safe, we add semester after semester to the school of life. Sometimes it's an easy A, but often it is a struggle. I bravely divorced my first husband in Hong Kong and then suffered the loss of my second husband of a heart attack after only five years of marriage. "Now what?" I questioned. As one friend said, "You have to decide if you are going to live." Well, now, that was a concept.

With the birth of my first grandchild, embracing life took on new meaning: suddenly I had a new lens through which to view the world, seeing everything again for the first time with the benefit of knowledge and wisdom. When I heard that an acquaintance in Honolulu would finish her MBA at the age of 57, I did the math and thought, "I could do that!" You may ask how such an idea would cross my mind, and my daughter put it very succinctly more than once: "Why can't you be a normal grandma?" What she didn't realize was that I had seen a copy of my own job description which read, "Excellent financial skills, knowledge of IRR, NPV; MBA a plus." Gulp! That announcement had been haunting me. I kept getting my AARP notices and applications for long-term care, but my goal was to qualify for the job I had been doing for 16 years.

My friends commiserated with me as I spent every other weekend in class, 1 to 6 on Friday and 8 to 6 on Saturday, overwhelmed with mounds of reading and papers to write. I picked up Johnny's doughnuts for the class every Saturday as a special treat to take the edge off. Now it has been only four weeks since I finished, and tell me I didn't say this—I kind of miss it. Not just the doughnuts, but the stimulation and the challenge. It gave me that same youthful feeling I get when I ride my bike.

"Now what?" a friend teased as she toasted me at the party she hosted and asked collectively, "Remember the thoughts that went through your mind when Kathleen said she was going back to school?" My only response was, "If you hear I am going for a Ph.D., shoot me." But you never know. . .

In this day and age of extended longevity, the possibilities are endless—what is a "normal" grandparent today? My friends are writing books, studying art, winning golf tournaments, dabbling in politics, selling real estate, and working out regularly. We are expanding our choices as we weave the fabric of our lives. First we lay the cross threads, the foundation, and then we experiment with the vertical threads, creating patterns on our road to somewhere.

PLEASURES AND PASTIMES

SINGING WITH THE OKAY CHORALE

Karen Yencich

I'VE ALWAYS SUNG, and I've always thought I was pretty good at it. Of course, now that I'm grown up, I know better. Meeting people who were truly excellent, I was forced to admit that I got the solo in the sixth-grade Christmas pageant not because I was the best, but because the teacher knew I was a ham and would never freeze in front of a crowd.

Later, in a big high school with serious performing groups where entrance was purely competitive, I came to understand that I made the cut mostly because I was dependable. I took singing seriously and was willing to submit to the rigorous discipline in order to—of course—perform.

Even though I loved singing, it was pretty clear, even to me, even then, that I had no future in music. Still, I managed to keep a tonsil in the game, singing in the church choir and later moving up to the Honolulu Symphony Chorus, an organization that required an audition only to assure itself that you weren't tone-deaf, and whose members once pitched a fit when it was suggested that they might wear shoes to perform.

Down the line, a husband and children conspired to keep me from performing, if not singing. A long time later, at a street fair, I saw a booth for a local community chorus and read the fateful words: "No audition required." Rehearsals for "Elijah" were underway, and although it was politely pointed out that what they really needed were male voices, I predictably failed to take the hint, and showed up for rehearsals the next night.

This might be a good time to point out that I can't actually read music; I've always memorized it. I've also relied on composers to be predictable, that is to say, keeping a lid on the sharps and flats and musical ornamentation. "Elijah" is a great slab of an oratorio, and Mendelssohn entertained himself by flinging sharps and flats about to create clever, unexpected chords when he might have easily left well enough alone. It's not as though, after a couple of hours, anyone was going to notice.

Two months later, suited up and stuffed to the gills with musical notations, I strode on stage. Singing in one of these events is a lot like riding a really big roller coaster, and I experience a small lurch of panic with the downbeat as the cars glide out of the station. There's no getting off now. "Helllllp Lord! Helllllp Lord!" we sing, gathering speed. The soloists plead. The chorus beats its collective breast, laboring up the first of many musical inclines. Elijah is advised to get out of town. Hark! He returns! He baits Ahab and the priests of Baal: we're rollin' now! Fire descends from heaven! Ahhhhhh! The chorus is in free fall! The tympanist goes nuts. The priests lose. Drought over. And it's only intermission. There's still Jezebel on the prowl, exile, despondency, reassurances, a whirlwind, additional disasters, and a fiery chariot ride into heaven. Amen! Amen! Amen! And the roller coaster that is "Elijah"—idols, mayhem, flaming chariots, floods, and blessings—swoops into the station, the audience bursts into applause, and the chorus files modestly into the wings.

In defense of community choruses everywhere, we're not the Mormon Tabernacle Choir. We are volunteers, often affiliated with a local community college or some other community group that helps foot the bills. We rehearse on our own time, after we've punched out at work, fed our kids, and raked the kitty litter. Some of us are tremendously accomplished, experienced performers with substantial talent. Others are serious singers, with fine voices, and the training to back them up. The rest of us are reliable and don't sound too bad most of the time. But what we all have in common is a passionate love of singing, whether it's classical, jazz, show tunes, or a cappella music. Whatever you've got, somebody out there loves singing it and is betting that somebody else wants to hear it.

Community choruses sing the people's music. You don't need to mortgage the house to attend a performance—admission is always a bargain, often it's free. You won't have to travel far to hear one of them; there are probably performances in your community, or the next town over. And the concerts are congenial—usually you'll run into friends and neighbors at these events, or even better, recognize them on the stage. Performers especially are foolishly grateful for your interest, which is a good thing to remember when, later on, you want someone to pick up the mail while you're on vacation.

Since "Elijah," I've swooned with Fauré, and snuffled through the pitifully touching Mozart *Requiem*, the latter just in time for a second performance as part of an international commemoration of the deaths at the World Trade Center. I've sung in French, Italian, Hebrew, German, and Latin, so much Latin that I'm beginning to understand it. Schubert! Lauridsen! Beethoven! Bloch and Barber! Stravinsky! I've had my moments with all of them.

Haydn's *Lord Nelson Mass* is next. A rather ebullient composer, Haydn spent a lot of time in his oratorio, *The Creation*, yelling, getting the string section to sound like bugs, and swanning about like a teenager over Adam and Eve. So considering that Admiral Nelson died in battle at sea, and was thoughtfully preserved in a barrel of rum by his crew so that he could be returned to England for burial, I'm looking forward to something pretty rousing. Hey, I could get you a great deal on tickets.

HOW TO SPICE UP YOUR LIFE

Elizabeth Fishel

FOR YEARS OUR FAMILY DINNER MENU was as regimented as the Buckingham palace guards. Monday nights, pasta; Tuesday, fish; Wednesday, chicken; Thursday, tacos; Friday, chicken apple sausages. Weekends I declared the kitchen closed and offered my husband the option of rustling up something for us himself or going out.

We'd slipped into this routine by default when our two sons were younger and fussier, and I knew which tried-and-true favorites they were guaranteed to eat. No recipes required, no six o'clock panic about what to cook.

Then the boys became teenagers, their tastes and horizons expanded, and our life as a family moved to a new stage. Each of us in our own way was hungry for reinvention.

Let other moms pierce their noses, take up the tango, or run away with their yoga instructors. To turn up the sizzle in my life, I decided to spice up my cooking with a Thai cooking class taught by chef and cookbook author Chat Mingkwan at a culinary supply store.

In Sur La Table's demonstration kitchen, seductive smells and exotic ingredients beckoned—bowls of glistening limes and lemons, bottles of luscious-colored liquids (passion-red fish sauce, mahogany-dark soy sauce), watermelons carved to look like lotus blossoms. Their sensuality whispered promises of transformation. Here I could surely shed my outer Betty Crocker to reveal the mistress of spices within.

Our group of 15 settled on two rows of chairs, sipping wine or thick, sweet Thai iced tea. Among us were a very pregnant mom, a midlife father and his eager, 20-something daughter, a tech-whiz whose wife wanted him to pull more weight in the kitchen. Was I just projecting or was each of us at a crossroads, each hoping for more than a culinary makeover? Anyway, the class was entertaining, and Chat, a consummate showman as he led us on a cook's tour of Thai dishes, his every slice and flourish reflected in huge mirrors overhead.

As the crepe is to the French and spaghetti to the Italians, pad thai is the signature dish of Thai cooking. It's an adaptation of the classic Chinese noodle stir-fry, introduced by trade in the 17th century and liberally seasoned by Thai cooks who found the Chinese version tasty but too bland. Chat demonstrated the zesty, distinctive blend of ingredients that makes the dish such a crowd-pleaser: the sweet (a sprinkling of sugar), the sour (vinegar), and the salty (shrimp, chopped peanuts, and fish sauce, the sine qua non of Thai cooking). These key ingredients plus handfuls of vegetables, soft slices of tofu, and velvety scrambled eggs are stir-fried quickly in a wok over high heat and served on a comforting bed of rice noodles. "Seven minutes to cook," he teased, "and a lifetime to perfect."

The ingredients were set out on butcher block tables, pre-chopped and pre-measured, so that we could toss the dish together with a TV chef's finesse, while Chat coached us: "More sugar! Add some water to keep it moist!" Announcing that he'd "grade" us on presentation as well as taste and technique, he inspired dishes decorated with tiny orchids and garnished with lime wedges and slivered red peppers in eye-popping patterns. So long to my days of serving straight from pot to table.

Trying the recipe at home the next week, preparing everything solo and from scratch, I found that the chopping became a soothing meditation as I contemplated the unfolding of my exciting new life. And the hodgepodge medley of flavors was so forgiving that when I added in the sauce too late, it didn't seem to matter. I was already learning to improvise, and the exotic seasonings infused the house with a perfume of possibility so intoxicating, I vowed I'd never fall back on Wednesday night chicken again. The boys declared the dish "awesome," and I swear my husband saw me with new eyes.

Tonight pad thai, tomorrow belly-dancing or the *Kama Sutra*?

A RECIPE FOR LOVE

Maureen Martin Appel

WITH THE RECENT PASSING of my 80-year-old godmother, I am immersed in mother memory, full of thoughts of all of the women I have borrowed for my own.

One woman stands out as a luminary on my makeshift mother line: my Aunt Marge, the lovely Margaret Anne Shaw, my father's baby sister. More than anyone else in my family, my Aunt Marge clearly desired and assumed the role of beloved grand-aunt to her nine nieces and nephews. From my earliest memories, she was busy gathering the family together for summer picnics, all the way back to the 1960s. At the old Shaw Ranch in Rutherford, California (with the dark barn still visible from the highway today), she hosted warm, unhurried summer meals under the trellised grape arbor, my father and uncles and aunts laughing and talking, chickens squawking, heat radiating across the valley floor. The cool dark interior of the old ranch house offered respite from the August sun, and I would stretch out on the faded sofa in the family room, with the ceiling fan turning quietly above me. There I'd read *Little Women* while my brothers and sister and cousins swam in the pool or shot their BB guns down at the creek.

In the summer of 1963 my aunt and uncle invited my siblings and me for an extended visit. My parents had been divorced for three years, and I was very attached to my mother. I hated leaving her, no matter what novelty and warmth awaited us in the country. In a fit of melancholy and desperately missing my mother, I sequestered myself in my cousin's bedroom and refused lunch. I was 11, shy, sensitive, and serious. In the midst of my sorrow my aunt appeared, gently sat down on the bed, and pulled out a small *Cookbook for Boys and Girls* from her large apron pocket. She asked if I would like to make something with her in the kitchen.

I slowly paged through that magical book filled with vivid color pictures, and chose a recipe called "Eggs in a Frame" with a picture of an egg, sunny side up, neatly cooked in the perfectly hollowed-out center of a piece of bread. We assembled all of the ingredients, just the two of us, pressing out the circle of bread with the lip of a small clear glass and carefully buttering the slice of bread, both top and bottom, then cracking the egg into the hole, and watching everything sizzle in the small cast-iron skillet. She sat with me as I ate my late lunch, offering herself to me that afternoon, filling in so sweetly for the mother I was missing.

My mother passed away shortly after that summer. Although a fair distance separated Marge from the rest of my family, she continued to show up for every important event—my graduations, my wedding party, our first home, the birth and baptism of each of our children. She and my uncle came bearing gifts—her smile, a box of chocolates, cookies, wine, books. They almost never failed to offer great encouragement, although every now and again she would surprise me with frankness. "Maureen, those eyeglasses are too heavy for your face," she announced over lunch one day. "You need a lighter, prettier frame."

I've had a lot of time to study Aunt Marge. She has made it her priority not only to stay connected to her extended family, but to nourish and feed us with a steady stream of loving-kindnesses. "You're doing a great job!" she writes at the end of her hand-written notes. "Your mother and father would be so proud of you." I realize suddenly that I don't have one favorite recipe from her, unless there is a recipe for *love*. The physical act of cooking is not what brings her the most pleasure (although she is a very capable cook), but the magnanimous feeding of her family. Hers is a larger recipe for living, and one that has clearly imprinted itself in my mind:

Shower the people you love with love.
Guaranteed to serve any family well.

I LOVE A PIANO
(AFTER IRVING BERLIN'S TUNE COMPOSED FOR "STOP, LOOK, & LISTEN," 1915)

Patty Northlich

IT WAS A MOMENTOUS MOVE from my parents' walk-up studio in Brooklyn to a spacious one-bedroom flat in Queens. In 1943, after eight years of marriage, they needed room for two life-changing arrivals. One was me. The other was a precious gift from my young accountant father to my mother, a Knabbe spinet piano, which he bought on time over two years.

"Stardust" and scales filled the air. My mother accompanied dance classes in local lofts, where she was paid 35 cents to $1.00 an hour. I loved to lie on my back in bed before falling asleep at night, and walk my feet up and down the wallpapered bedroom wall from rose to rose in time to the music.

In the fall five years later, we relocated to Dobbs Ferry in Westchester County. Our two-story house came with a brilliant maple tree pushing up through the front porch, space for the spinet in the living room, an additional bedroom for a baby sister, and a neighborhood of musicians, including Burl Ives.

The doorbell chimed one sultry morning the following summer. My mother received a telegram. In a Norman Rockwell–like domestic scene of the late '40s, she stood at the screen door in her blue-flowered house dress with white apron tied around the waist, calico cat and two young daughters at her feet peering up at her as she read the message. Breaths were held. A fly buzzed. My mother's quizzical frown was replaced with her usual pretty expression. At last she explained.

After high school she had attended Oberlin Conservatory of Music to study piano. This was only possible because she had been awarded the prestigious Edward Drummond Libby Scholarship from Libby Glass Company in her hometown of Toledo, Ohio. She attributed her achievement largely to her music teacher, Sue Love. The telegram said that Sue Love had died, and when her will was read, my mother was named to inherit Sue's Steinway Grand Piano. The piano in its original cover would arrive the following week.

Suddenly, my mother scurried into our living room where the Knabe piano took up most of the inner wall. She walked around, looked up and down, and then declared: "The Steinway will go in the dining room." The day the Steinway was hoisted up on the porch, knocking a branch off the maple tree, and angled through the front door, dining table and chairs were moved to the sun room. The dining room was exactly where the Steinway went.

Overnight, life changed. My mother played the Steinway constantly, opening the flood gates to a steady stream of troubadours—the boisterous glee club who gathered around the Steinway for rehearsals; three bustling ladies sporting hats with feathers, who came to practice intricate classical two-piano pieces; and neighbors of all ages, responding to my mother's invitations for sing-along parties on folding chairs, featuring our famous pink punch in paper cups.

My father's muse arrived. He composed score and lyrics for his masterwork, dedicated to my mother and titled "Jane," my mother's name. My grandmother undertook a two-year task of needlepointing a canvas painted with musical instruments against a turquoise-colored background to cover the piano-bench lid. My favorite pastime was dancing to my mother's playing, a ballerina in flight, executing grand jetés off the round, yellow-leather fringed hassock, which sat next to the Steinway.

Often my mother performed locally. I remember drama and glamour before she departed—the rustle of black taffeta, her sparkling jewelry, the shiny red nail polish, the scent of Joy perfume wafting behind her. When she was in her eighties, she cut a master tape of standards, including "Jane." She sold the recordings, netting several thousand dollars, which she donated to a foundation. Her soft touch, still sure today, reminds me of a comment by Austrian-American pianist Artur Schnabel: "The notes I handle no better than many pianists. But the pauses between the notes—ah, that is where the art resides."

Half a century since she received her gift, my mother, now 93, still plays her Steinway. The piano is in the dining room of her apartment in Scottsdale, Arizona. She plays only by ear since her vision is dimmed by macular degeneration. She also plays the piano in the dining room of the residence where she lives. She is a popular entertainer who can play almost any request from Bach fugues to University fight songs. Hawaiian print dresses have replaced the black taffeta; her fingers are curved with arthritis, but her nails are still beautifully painted with "Love That Red."

My 29-year-old son shares the relative pitch of my mother. He composed eleven piano etudes in his grandmother's honor in the recital for his Master's in Music Composition at New York University. On a recent summer evening, I overheard the two of them swinging on the front porch glider, discussing the key in which they thought our resident mockingbird was chirping.

My mother has told me that I will inherit her Steinway. I have paperwork on the piano, which includes its serial number and "birth date" of December 10, 1924 in the New York factory. It is a Steinway M Vintage piano, which means that it was built between 1900 and 1960. I consider it a great honor and responsibility to inherit the Steinway, and am hoping that it will fit in my California dining room.

I feel a certain confidence because I have already had a little practice of my own with a Steinway piano delivery. It came one afternoon when I was at my post as Concierge of a large San Francisco Bay Area resort. A VIP guest and cabaret star contacted me at the Concierge desk to say that his Steinway would be arriving and would I please see that it got placed safely in his guestroom?

"No problem," I said. "I understand your concerns. I have a Steinway in my family."

OBJECTS OF DESIRE

Trish Hawthorne

SOMETIMES I DROP BY THE SHOP just to admire them. Even if I can never have them for my own, it's a pleasure to know where I can find them. There they are in the upper left-hand corner of the glass case, beautiful as ever. I don't look at the other gems on display; my eye goes straight to the familiar spot. The crystals dusting their surfaces catch the light, highlighting their rich amber glow. I love their generous roundness, the way a few random cracks break the smoothness. Perfection!

I'm not visiting a jewelry store, although the parallel has crossed my mind. My destination is a small bakery, where the merchandise is just as precious as jewels and even more delicious. The objects of my desire are not brooches or beads, not pearls or pendants, but treasures nonetheless. The glowing vision in the glass case, the stuff of which my dreams are made, is the humble gingersnap.

Of course, these gingersnaps are far from humble. I fell in love at first bite. They're dense and chewy, dark and spicy, with a peppery snap that lingers on the tongue.

Some rich blend of molasses, ginger, and perhaps a bit of mustard makes them fragrant and mysterious. They are the best of the breed. After my first taste a few years ago, I wanted nothing more than to be able to re-create these wonders myself.

It seemed simple at the time. I asked the young woman behind the counter if the recipe was available. She sighed; she had obviously been asked this question before. No, she told me, the baker never gave out the recipe for the gingersnaps. The scowling face of the owner, who appeared suddenly from the back room, made it clear that this recipe was a trade secret. I was disappointed but not discouraged, confident that I'd find the right recipe in my cookbooks at home.

So I searched through my cookbooks and baked more batches of gingersnaps than I can even recall. I've made dozens of delicious cookies, and in the process learned a lot about the many variations on the gingersnap theme. They can be thin and crisp, delicate and ladylike, teatime food from *The Joy of Cooking*. They can be wholesome and steadfast, like the ones found in *Comfort Food*, perfect solace for a friend who needs some cheer. They can have amusing names, like the "Elevator Lady Spice Cookies" in the *I Hate to Cook Book*. I discovered a bond with the food writer M.F.K. Fisher when I read that she made gingersnaps often. After baking the recipe I found in one of her books, I knew that she liked the crispy type, and added lots of ground ginger to get an extra zing. The recipes I've collected may call for fresh or crystallized ginger, for unsulfured molasses, for white pepper or instant coffee, for margarine or butter. But so far I've been unable to reproduce the dark and chewy cookies with the tantalizing blend of spices I crave.

It seems I'm not the only one who is passionate about this particular gingersnap. In asking around, I learned that the recipe had once been cause for litigation. The owner of the bakery I frequent used to have a business partner. When they parted company, there was a lively dispute over who would get custody of the gingersnaps. It took lawyers to determine that both bakers could use the recipe, but in different locations, thus eliminating competition. Even though both women still live in the same town, one now ships her cookies elsewhere for sale. No wonder my request for the recipe was met with a scowl.

My discovery of the "mail order" cookies provided yet another clue. Those cookies had the ingredients listed right on the package. Now I know to use shortening rather than butter, and to add crystallized ginger. This moved me closer to getting the right result, but it still didn't produce the perfect cookie.

The recipe I seek may be as unattainable as the holy grail. But my search has become even more fun than eating those chewy gingersnaps, so on I go. And to sustain myself, every so often I pay a quick visit to the bakery to gaze fondly at the objects of my desire. The gingersnaps shimmer in the glass case, resting comfortably next to a saucy lemon tart.

SWIRL, SNIFF, SIP, SPIT

Linda Goldfarb

SWIRL, SNIFF, SIP, SPIT. Swirl, sniff, sip, spit.

What are we doing here?

My husband and I and ten other people, all somehow connected to the wine industry, are sitting around a long, wooden table in our neighbor's St. Helena dining room. Six partially-filled wine glasses are lined up in a row in front of each of us. Next to the last glass at each setting sits a solitary red plastic cup. One by one, we pick up each glass and swirl the wine around, bring it to the nose, and draw a big inhalation. Then the glass is silently and ceremoniously placed down. This ritual is repeated with the remaining glasses. Finally, we raise each glass, sip the wine, and spit it out into the plastic cups. Once the wine in each glass has been swirled, sniffed, sipped, and spit, the silence is broken.

"I'm getting almond extract and dark berries on the nose," Wendy says, as she deftly swirls her first glass.

"Yes, yes, and a bit of orange cassis and spice—wait, and tobacco, there's definitely tobacco," Rob adds, barely able to contain his excitement.

"Leather and licorice in the mid-palate," Joe says in his typical serious manner. "But the tannins, way over the top, wouldn't you say?" He looks up at the group for approval. They all nod as Leslie motions with her glass and says, "And the finish, what the heck happened with that?!"

I swear these are actual conversations that have taken place at the monthly wine-tasting group that my husband and I attend. I say "attend," as "participate" would imply that in some way we contribute something—anything—to the group. We don't. We try to lie low and not embarrass ourselves.

Three years ago, my husband and son and I moved to the wine country to escape our daily 15-mile, two-hour commute to San Francisco. We hoped to find a slower but more fulfilling way of life. Our St. Helena home sat on a small piece of property that came with a half acre of cabernet grapevines—149 to be exact. Not wanting the grapes to rot on the vines, my husband and I decided to try to make wine ourselves, never imagining the road this decision would lead us down. Using knowledge gained from reading intellectual books such as *Winemaking for Dummies*, and talking to anyone who knew more than we did on the subject, which turned out to be most everyone, we started making wine.

"You need to join a wine-tasting group," we heard over and over. "That's the best way to learn. Just ask around, you'll find one."

So we asked around. Most of the people we had met in the wine community were in at least one or more tasting groups. These groups varied in size and form from small groups of four to very large, formal groups of up to 20. Some met in homes, others in restaurants or any place that would accommodate them. Every kind of wine imaginable was fair game. Most groups tasted varietals from various wine-producing countries like France, Italy, Spain, and Australia. Some groups were more specialized, tasting only California wines. Some were even more specific, tasting only California cabernets, but most groups varied their "juice" choices. We quickly learned that "juice" was not just a descriptor for non-alcoholic drinks. Parents, watch out if your teenagers tell you they drank only "juice" at parties.

A few months into our search, we were asked if we would like to join our neighbors' group, as one couple had dropped out. We soon realized that either you create your own group (and good luck finding someone who isn't already in one), or you are asked to join an existing group. The one we were asked to join had been meeting for 12 years. I suppose we should have felt honored; instead, we just felt pressure. Could we, the amateurs, fake our way with these professionals?

At our first tasting, the host had chosen a Tempranillo (huh?) from the Priorat (where?) region of Spain. Most of the group members were winemakers, vineyard managers, or winery owners. They used words like "dark fruit" as well as "rotten eggs" to describe the wines we tasted. All the bottles were hidden in brown paper bags to disguise their origins so as not to prejudice our palates. We learned that the "finish" is of utmost importance when drinking wine. You do not want a finish that is "short" or "tannic" or "tight" but rather one that tastes "long" and "silky" and "smooth."

We learned that wine can taste like a "barnyard" or even like "wet stone" (which is supposedly a good thing). I, for one, have never tasted a wet stone, or a barnyard, so I'd be hard pressed to comment on a wine that resembles such places or things.

I'd have no problem if asked to describe chocolate—but wine? Not a chance. We thought that with time, we'd get the hang of these descriptive phrases, or at least come up with a core set that would get us through the evening. "It tastes pretty good" was the best we could muster without calling attention to ourselves.

As each year passed, we learned more about winemaking and eventually found a real winemaker to help us make a wine we could actually sell. Our vocabulary of descriptors had grown, but still, we struggled to describe our wine. Although "Yum, it tastes good" was succinct and to the point, we didn't think it would be received in the spirit it was intended. We were getting ready to release our first vintage and knew that we were expected to produce "tasting notes" to describe the wine.

We scoured wine publications, reading the descriptions used to entice oenophiles to purchase wine: "Mulberry, cassis, open and airy texture, racy structure. . . ." The more we read, the more we were convinced that the words were repetitive and that there was a basic set of adjectives for cabernets, a set for chardonnays, etc. And then we wondered, do people really read and pay attention to these descriptions?

So we came up with a paragraph that we felt aptly described cabernet—I mean our cabernet. But I wanted to test my theory. Around that time, Starbucks had come out with an intense chocolate drink called "Chantico." I liked the sound of that word. Even though, technically, the word described the Aztec goddess of home and hearth, since it was used in conjunction with a chocolate drink, I could make the argument that our wine went well with chocolate, hence the connection.

So in the middle of the flowery paragraph describing our wine, I wrote: "Essence of Chantico flows through the mid-palate."

Would anyone notice this strange word in the midst of our prose? Our release letter, along with the tasting notes, was mailed to the 1,500 people on our mailing list. And how many contacted us to find out exactly what Chantico meant? Two.

It's been three years since we released our wine. We still attend the monthly tasting group and still try not to make comments that are too inappropriate. It may be the power of suggestion, but we think we have tasted a hint of chocolate in our cabernet. As for that important "finish"—it's right here. Chantico!

TRAVELS

AN ANGEL IN BAHIA

Terri Hinte

BAHIA: the most African region of Brazil. The wellspring of Brazilian spiritual life. Home of novelist Jorge Amado and composer Dorival Caymmi. I knew I had to include it in my itinerary—specifically its capital city, Salvador. My Portuguese teacher Ana, in the Bay Area, agreed that it was a wonderful destination. But she visibly recoiled when I told her I wanted to stay near Pelourinho Square, the oldest and most picturesque part of the city and the very site where slaves were once auctioned and pilloried (*pelourinho* translates as "whipping post"). The modern Pelourinho district was home to artists and musicians but was also poor, and by some accounts dangerous. Ana looked at me gravely. "You must absolutely *not* stay in the Pelourinho," she warned. "It's not for American tourists."

That settled that. I would stay in the Pelourinho.

Next decision: what was the one thing I *had* to do while in Bahia? What would make my visit definitive, unforgettable? I peppered friends and music business associates with inquiries, Americans and Brazilians who had spent time there. To my amazement, five people I'd polled who were only marginally acquainted with one another each told me: "You must go to the Cantina da Lua and meet Clarindo Silva." That amounted to a divine dictum, an order from on high.

Situated like a fortress on a cliff overlooking the Bay of All Saints, Salvador had for 250 years been Brazil's crown jewel, its seat of wealth and government and its chief port of entry. Due east across the Atlantic was Angola, which shares a complex, difficult, yet vibrant history with Bahia, most of whose citizens are the descendants of African slaves.

I arrived in Salvador right after Christmas, planning to stay a few days and get back to Rio by New Year's. My hotel, the Pelourinho (the whipping post!), was a charming colonial structure on a narrow cobblestone street just off the historic square.

Jorge Amado had once lived there, according to a plaque in the lobby. I knew from his books—like *Dona Flor and Her Two Husbands* and *Tent of Miracles*—that Bahians were on intimate terms with the sea and with unseen forces: their gods and angels and spirits were alive, and exerted a tangible influence on the smallest details of an individual's day-to-day strivings.

Once settled into my room, I realized that I didn't have a map of the city, didn't even have an address or phone for the sought-after Cantina da Lua ("Moon Canteen"). I nevertheless took off for an impromptu walk in the neighborhood. Standing at the hotel's front door, I saw the square, the Largo do Pelourinho, a hundred feet to my left. I walked up to it and spotted another narrow street that forked off from the plaza, running somewhat parallel to the noisy, bustling tributary on which my hotel was located. It was there I headed for my afternoon stroll.

Despite its proximity to the street I was staying on, this quiet little *rua* I now found myself exploring was a world apart. There were some intermittent cobblestones underfoot as I began my walk; these quickly disappeared. The road was unpaved, just parched and pocked dirt.

This was a residential area, car-free and not a business or storefront in sight. A few shoeless children were playing. Here and there a lean clucking chicken, scavenging crumbs. A skinny dog skulking across my path. A couple of shabby men smoking, several others bantering, looking at me. Eyes on me. Suddenly I realized I should not be there. I'd been walking for perhaps five minutes and ahead of me I could detect no outlet, no intersection, only this godforsaken alley stretching out forever. It was too late to turn around—conspicuous. Couldn't run—where? I was carrying money, passport, a camera even—what an idiot. Not to mention my sun-bleached blondness, as subtle as a klieg light in a darkened theater—the only blond in the Pelourinho. Almost imperceptibly I felt the men on the street turn menacing, preparing to approach me with no peaceful purpose.

At that moment there was a fluttering around the back of my head, an audible displacement of air, like the *whoosh* of a very large flapping wing. I seemed to be floating along in a cocoon, as down a river, and the people outside of it appeared as a faint, fading image on a screen. Then—after some seconds? minutes?— the cocoon fell away, and I looked up and saw a church: I'd reached, at last, the end of the street, which opened on to a large parklike square where a crafts fair was taking place.

As I wandered among the booths, breathing easily, I heard a man's voice behind me. He was addressing me as if we knew each other: "Here, this looks like it would fit you fine," he said, holding up a gauzy peasant-style blouse with turquoise embroidery. I beheld a handsome man with cocoa-brown skin and a bewitching smile—Geraldo. At first he thought I was from the south of Brazil—where all the Germans are—but once he learned I was from California he was eager to play host.

"So Teresa, what do you want to do while you're in Bahia?"

"I want to go to the Cantina da Lua and meet Clarindo Silva." My mission.

Geraldo gave a start, then turned around and gestured grandly with an open arm. We were standing right in front of the Cantina da Lua!

"Let's go meet Clarindo," he said, taking my arm as we crossed the street. "He's a good friend of mine."

The Cantina was a busy, friendly neighborhood hangout/ bar/eatery where I immediately felt at home. As we took a table in a nook off the sunny main room, Geraldo flagged down a waiter and ordered two ice-cold beers, the only proper drink for a 95-degree afternoon. Then he went off to find Clarindo, and returned with the Cantina's world-renowned proprietor: a compact, wiry man whose face gave the impression that it was accustomed to registering delight. He had an inviting manner and an easy charisma—a born host. Clarindo grasped my hands as we were introduced, and took great pleasure in hearing the names of our mutual acquaintances. "*Fique à vontade!*" he exclaimed; we were to make ourselves comfortable. The drinks, of course, were on him.

My ostensible mission accomplished, I turned my attention to the handsome man sharing my table. Geraldo was a real talker, but I had no trouble understanding his Portuguese. In the two or three hours we spent in the Cantina, we exchanged bits and pieces of our histories. He worked as a mechanical engineer, and was a percussionist in his spare time; only a few years earlier, he'd spent a year in New York, my hometown.

Geraldo was very taken with me and pitched his woo with a tender ardor. "You're very *parecida* with Brazil," he kept saying— I really fit in, that is. "You ought to come live here for um tempo *bastante*"—a good long while. (With him, of course!) This was unlikely to happen; but I let him work his spell on me.

Ours was a sweet romance. We shone for each other. He loved showing me his city at night: we drove past the vast dark beaches and the churches blazing with light, including the beautiful Our Lord of Bonfim's, where we saw a joyous wedding party spilling out onto the street. We stopped by the Boa Viagem beach and happened upon elaborate preparations for the year-end maritime procession honoring Lord Jesus of the Sailors. He pointed out neighborhoods I'd be ill-advised to visit unescorted, and took me to a bar reminiscent of New York, where we sipped rum cocktails and held hands.

I didn't move to Bahia to live with Geraldo. Perhaps I might have upended my life if circumstances at home had been only slightly different, if certain plans I'd been tending were not already sprouting and taking root. We wore sad smiles when we parted on the morning of New Year's Eve, saying *até logo* (see you soon), promising letters, even a visit in California. None of that came to pass.

Instead I was left with a small supply of *fitas* he'd given me. These brightly colored ribbons, often imprinted with the words "Remembrance of Our Lord of Bonfim," are worn by most Bahians (and many other Brazilians) as talismans. A ribbon is tied on the wrist and knotted three times, with a wish made on each knot, then left in place till the *fita* disintegrates and falls off. (Bad luck will result if the ribbon is cut prematurely.) According to an embellishment told to me by a Rio friend, you must then take the tattered remains of the *fita* and set it in a body of running water, ideally an ocean, whereupon your wishes will come true.

As I worked my way through the stock of *fitas*, I made many wishes, variations on the usual themes of health, wealth, and happiness. Sometimes, caught up in the daily grind, I was too busy to notice whether the wishes were being granted, but the sight of the fraying ribbon on my wrist always gently tugged at my heart. One day nearly three years after my trip to Bahia, my final *fita* came undone. Dutifully I drove to Rodeo Beach, just west of the Golden Gate Bridge, with the tiny faded-red rag on the seat beside me. It was typically windy and cold at the beach, and dozens of brown pelicans were expertly diving for their lunch. I walked up to the water's edge and tossed the *fita* into the crashing surf of the Pacific, which instantly claimed it.

When I arrived home, there was a postcard awaiting me. It was from Clarindo Silva, who was writing to tell me: "Your spirit is strongly felt in Bahia."

I could only reply: the spirit of Bahia is strong in me. I didn't write him, but I know he got the message.

IN MONET'S GARDEN

Christy Myers

"Color is my day-long obsession, joy, and torment." —Claude Monet

THE SMOOTH HIGHWAY follows the river Seine through small, quaint French villages and along stretches of curving flat water that reflects golden green poplar trees and old stone buildings bordering its banks. As the pretty scenes sweep by the car window, I remember paintings by Monet I've seen in museums of those same shimmering silver and gold trees mirrored in the glassy waters of the Seine.

I am finally having my long-awaited artist pilgrimage to Giverny—the home, garden, and water-lily ponds created by Claude Monet, the father of Impressionist painting. Monet lived here for 43 years until his death in 1926. A part of me hates visiting where someone had a wonderful life long ago, a life I would have loved, where now people are tromping daily. But as my chance to see it nears, my excitement builds. I hope I too will be able to sit and paint in the gardens.

My husband Ken and I arrive at Giverny, 50 miles northwest of Paris, and find a meadow of long grasses, red poppies, and blue bachelor buttons. It appears to be the spot where Monet painted his famous *Coquelicots* or *Wild Poppies* in 1873. Scattered in the grass in front of us are old-fashioned wood and iron folding tables and chairs; we decide to sit and soak in the scene. I cannot resist the pull to paint. While I unpack my painting supplies, Ken waits patiently with great anticipation of all before us yet to see.

As I learn more about seeing, I realize that each bush or tree, building or street, person or animal is not made up of just one color, *trees equal green*, but of subtle combinations of that hue. There is cadmium, alizarin, crimson, vermillion, and magenta in the red of the poppies before me.

Ken tries to read a Grisham paperback, but the legs of his tiny chair keep sinking into the soft ground. "This isn't working, sweetie, are you almost ready?" he says cautiously, knowing that my passion is to paint. Finally I give in to my curiosity. I temporarily quit on the poppy field and pack my things. We walk into the town of Giverny past houses and a few cute shops swathed in roses. One long dwelling on the opposite side of the road is painted in apple-green and trimmed in rose-pink, the distinctive color combination I've seen in photos of Monet's house.

Once inside the grounds, it is truly Monet's world. First we visit the gardens stretching out in front of his house and its long verandah. Outdoor corridors paved with pale beige crushed granite lead us sweeping downward between long rectangular flower beds. It's more a varied English garden than an ordered French one. Mauve-pink poppies with black centers stand tall like four-foot-high sentinels scattered above the other flowers. Arbors draped with different varieties of climbing roses surround us in shades of magenta, rose, and peach.

Amongst the pink fuchsias, orange rununculas, blue bachelor buttons, and white daisies march large groups of five-year-old French children with their teachers. They are chattering and sometimes singing together, each child wearing an adorable hat. Obviously their mothers had been told, "They must have a hat!"

Ken and I sit on a carved stone bench for a while just basking in the bright sunny day. Birds are also singing; butterflies and bees make their rounds. The country air is sweet with the scent of flowers, firs, and rich humus soil. There are crowds, but in the respites between groups, I imagine what it was like when Monet painted one of his canvases here.

Steps to a tunnel take us under the one-lane road that separates Monet's garden from his water lily ponds. We walk the paths around the ponds. There are places to sit and contemplate forest vignettes with hostas and ferns. Stretching in a lazy arch across the far end of the ponds is the famous green bridge covered in lavender wisteria that graces so many of Monet's paintings. Soft trees and foliage frame the scene. Between us and the bridge are the floating islands of water lilies, pods yellow-green except where the leaves curl up to expose their cerulean-blue underside.

I look at what Monet saw and imagine that the trees and blue sky reflected in the water full of lily pods must be what caught his eye. I set out my watercolors to paint, and Ken pulls out his spy novel. I begin, not expecting much of myself, mostly to know that I have painted in Monet's garden. Between me and the scene before me are long dark strands of weeping willow hanging from the tree rooted behind us. I'm looking deep into Monet's vision. It's this layer upon layer that is so intriguing to paint: the dark tendrils of willow leaves hanging in front of the lily pods, set in the reflection of the trees, with the bridge, its wisteria, and the sky and clouds beyond.

As I paint, periods of quiet bliss are interrupted by the voices of the schoolchildren tramping by with their teachers. "*Très jolie*," "*Plantes, fleurs.* . ." These crowds I enjoy. One petite teacher, about 25 in shiny black pants and a gypsy off-the-shoulders top, stops her dozen charges and sits them on the ground next to Ken and me to "paint" like Monet with primary marker pens. Speaking only French, the children show great admiration for the beauty around them. "*Oh, très imaginatif, mon petit*," their *professeur* says, tossing her curls as they show her their drawings. She asks to borrow my painting and holds it up for the children to see. One blond munchkin comes up to me and begins a long diatribe, assuming I speak French.

"*Très jolie*," very pretty, he says as he points to my painting and tells me on and on in French about his painting. The cute teacher winks.

"*Oh, oui, oui*," I say in the appropriate pauses as the little boy looks up at me with complete innocent sincerity in his bright green eyes. Ken smiles at me; he's as charmed as I am. The glow of Giverny has bathed us in a sweet calm.

TIRAMISU OR S'MORES

Joan Stevenson

MY LOVE AFFAIR WITH ITALY began many years ago when I went
camping with my children. I would remind them as I slaved over
a Coleman stove to make hot dogs and chili interesting that one
day I would vacation in a villa in Florence and sleep covered with
a fluffy down comforter, far from the musty green regulation army
tent, the sleeping bag, and the air mattress that predictably
deflated. Their reaction was tolerant and dismissive.

If there is any redemption on a camping vacation, it comes in
the early hours of the morning. When you rise at dawn welcomed
by the fragrance of the woods laced with the aroma of coffee, the
day has begun gloriously. Unfortunately it is a steady downhill
from there. The pancakes made by adding water to a powder mix
never grill to a golden brown. How can they when the control is
a fickle charcoal fire? On a camp vacation they are blackened on
the edges, raw in the middle, and drowning in fake maple syrup.
I feel as if I am working harder than ever. There is just a short
time between heating the water to do the breakfast dishes and
preparing the sandwiches for the backpacking lunch.

Last year as our plane swooped through the clouds, my eyes
beheld the patchwork of gardens and vineyards on the rolling
Tuscan hillside below. The vacation I had dreamed about from a
drafty tent decades ago was about to come true. My husband Bob
and I decided to combine a vacation in Italy with a cooking
school, La Cucina di Viviana (Vivian's Cooking School), three
miles outside Florence. Our trip included four nights as a guest in
her home, the 14th-century Villa Il Cerretino. We were met by
Vivian's cooking-school partner, Barbara, who already had our
classmates in tow—a newlywed couple from Albuquerque. (The
school takes only four students at a time.) Once we had stowed
our luggage in Vivian's van, we embarked on a quick tour of the
city. We moved through the streets crowded with other tourists,
crossing the famous Ponte Vecchio and on to the gardens of the

Pitti Palace. Finally Barbara maneuvered her car into the chaotic traffic of Florence, through the twisting narrow streets and up the hill to the villa where we would spend the next five days.

That night we were the guests, and the first course Vivian and Barbara served was a glorious pasta dish made with zucchini and garlic. Even that humble squash took on an air of class that made me rethink its role in my garden! Starting early the next day we plunged into creating a Tuscan meal. We started our preparations by shopping for ingredients. We began with wine from Fattoria Montagliari, a vineyard that first shipped Chianti wine to our country in 1620. We selected our meat from Dario Cecchini, the legendary butcher of Chianti, who treats his customers with local songs, snippets of Dante, and a market groaning with meaty delicacies. Much to my relief we passed on the tripe and rabbit, traditional fare of the region, and settled on chicken, sausage, and pork roast. The local farmers' market is open only from 8 to 1 so we went there early enough to have the pick of the produce. The most important lesson of the day emphasized "fresh." Herbs, bread, vegetables, cheese, and meat were purchased the day they were to be prepared.

The emphasis on "fresh" was a contrast to the preparations for feeding my brood out in the woods many years ago. Greens and fruits were preserved in the ice chest for as long as the heat did not melt the ice. I did take a touch of Italian cuisine with me to the campground: homemade pasta sauce frozen to help chill the ice chest and used just as it was about to thaw. I could smell it simmering and poured a glass of Chianti to celebrate while I waited for the water to boil. That takes a very long time at high altitudes. So I had a second glass of wine. There was an early evening chill, and the thought of my dinner fortified by the wine warmed me. It was the moment when the pasta was finally done that I discovered the strainer was in the cupboard at home. I was carefully holding a cover to let the boiling water drain out when the escaping steam overcame me, and I dropped the pasta in the dirt. I stared at it, considering my options.

In Italy our class began at 5:00 p.m. For three hours four of us labored under the scrutiny of Barbara and Vivian. We boned and stuffed a chicken, and prepared a very complicated timbalo, chicken liver crostini, simple but delectable soups, garnishes to add a festive touch to any entrée, and tiramisu. The timbalo was an elegant first-course dish prepared in a pastry-lined spring-form pan. Two layers of tomato sauce, rigatoni, béchamel sauce, and cheese were topped with pastry and decorated with rosebuds and leaves. Our campsite dessert did not resemble tiramisu, but the day would not have been complete without it. S'mores were standard fare, a high-sugar combination my kids loved. After roasting a marshmallow to gooey golden perfection, we sandwiched it between two graham crackers with a square of Hershey's milk chocolate. After dessert we strolled to the campfire to hear tales of the forest and sing camp songs. One evening we watched as a brown bear, looking as if he never missed a meal, picked up a cooler, tossed it against a towering redwood, and scavenged through the contents, picking and devouring the most savory.

Dinner in Italy was so civilized. By 8:15 we sat down to the mouthwatering meal that we had created, beginning with pasta in some form, followed by a meat course and the dessert. Dinner was slow, rich with conversation, wine, and guests. No one hurried. There was time to relish and enjoy. The days ended near midnight, and I gratefully climbed the three flights of stairs to my bed with its cozy down covers.

It has been 40 years since I finally stood my ground and announced that the family would have to camp without me. Time has softened the memory. My children remember with fondness our trips to Yosemite and I do, too. But a Tuscan villa has become a style to which I've grown accustomed.

THE HAIRCUT

Ellen Newman

I TAKE ONE LOOK IN THE MIRROR and am scared straight to the phone. With my thick curly hair sticking out all over, I look more orangutan or Papua chieftain than the *orang-barat* or Westerner that I am. I'm one month into a six-month stay in Indonesia, and my locks desperately need to be tamed. Time to take my chances in a Jakarta salon.

First call to Marilyn, the former cultural affairs reporter for AP in Paris, now an expat in Jakarta. I could live with a chic, curly cut like hers. "Your last haircut was in Paris. Oh, I see." Georgia, my neighbor in the Hotel Borobudur who speaks Indonesian with a North Carolina accent, was furious with the ladies at the hotel salon. "They didn't even cover the gray," she moans.

Next, I try Kaye, the Korean-born wife of the U.S. Embassy's public affairs rep. Kaye's golden highlights make her face glow. "Ya," she says Indonesian-style, "Roberto, the Italian guy, does my hair." When I call Ellie, my blond friend from Boston, via Colorado, Hong Kong, Korea, and Japan, for a second opinion, she warns me, "Don't go near Roberto. He's an *artiste*, a little tyrant. Roberto ruined my hair."

Instead, Ellie suggests Mil & Mat, the salon in Kemang, her South Jakarta neighborhood. "They're really nice," she reassures me. So I call. "Two-thirty would be just fine," a pleasant voice says. That leaves barely enough time for a quick shower and a gobbled sandwich before grabbing a cab. No slack left for an ATM stop. I am already late.

As the cab eases into the street, I check my cash one more time. The five 100,000-*rupiah* notes barely put a bump in the slim green taxi wallet I bought for our trip to Asia. We are here because my husband has been assigned to a USAID legal project in Jakarta, our first "posting," as seasoned expats say. Now swarms of motorbikes, some ferrying entire families, vroom past us like clouds of gnats snaking between the lanes of cars—loads of SUVs and multihued taxis. Buses ooze workers from every door, and clusters of orange, foul-smelling, three-wheeled Indian *baji* cabs clog the streets.

I obsessively glance at my watch as we round the grand fountain and Stalinist-style welcome statue at Plaza Indonesia. Even in good traffic, it will take at least 40 minutes from here. There's nothing to do but watch as Jakarta rolls past—a teeming patchwork of red-roofed *kampungs* or villages, impressive office towers, elegant hotels, bustling shopping malls, and local street-side food stalls. The scene is punctuated by the naked rebar of several unfinished office buildings, abandoned during the Asian monetary crisis of 1998, that stand like ghosts watching a new Indonesia emerge from founder Sukarno's nationalist fervor and dictator Soeharto's 30 years of repression.

Finally, the cab turns left into the Kemang area, a low-rise mixture of homes, restaurants, boutiques, galleries, shops, and salons that reminds me of West Hollywood. I'm late, but I'm here.

Rita, the pleasant voice on the phone, greets me in the lobby of the third-floor salon. Do I have the instructions? Like a rookie secret agent fumbling for the code, I rummage through my purse for the pink Rolodex card with my San Francisco colorist's secret formula for brunette. The notes, unintelligible to me, make perfect sense to Rita, who ushers me inside. I'm invited to change into a kimono-style top that turns out to be way too small. I feel like an overripe Brunhilde in a land of delicate flowers.

Sumi, who is going to cut my hair, comes by to check out my frizzy, dry orang-locks before they're saturated with color. She is quickly replaced by Oja, who starts to comb in the color that Rita mixed. With barely a nod of greeting, gentle hands slip off my sandals and place my feet in a plastic tub of warm water to begin my pedicure. Before I've realized what's going on, Eri arrives, placing a plastic stool on either side of me and a towel-covered pillow on my lap. There are no manicure tables in Jakarta salons.

Rimi, the pedicurist, holds up a small metallic packet. "Herbal," she says, looking for ways to ask me if I want to add it to the footbath. "*Berapa,* how much?" I ask in return. How far will my 500,000 *rupiah* actually go? The equivalent of about $55, it would barely cover the haircut at home, let alone the color. Certainly no manicure and pedicure on the side. And I must remember to save enough for tips and the cab ride home. Credit cards, my usual savior when cash is low, are off-limits in Indonesia, with its reputation for rampant credit-card fraud. "Twenty thousand," she says. "OK," I reply, with a quiver in my stomach, trusting that the additional two dollars won't break the wallet.

"Would Madame like some tea?" offers yet another attendant in an orchid-pink polo shirt, the tidy yet feminine salon uniform. I take a moment to look around. My neighbor at the next chair is an Indonesian woman dressed in traditional long pants with a matching tunic, all in a pale green with embroidery framing her wrists and ankles. She is having a "cream bath," a conditioning treatment and head and shoulder massage that is an Indonesian specialty.

A cup of syrupy, thick ginger tea arrives just as Rimi pours the green herbal granules into her hand and starts to rub my feet and massage my legs. Bliss nudges aside my haircut anxieties until she bumps into one of the knots left over from my three-day study tour of West Java. Suddenly I'm back traversing the crater of Papandayan, one of Java's 40-plus active volcanoes, with a group of six women from six different countries. Deftly probing, she finds my tight Achilles, the aftershock of climbing down 350 steep steps to a traditional Sundanese village with its thatched roofs, communal outdoor shower, and—why am I not surprised—satellite dish. As Rimi's rhythmic strokes move on to my calves, I'm back on the bus rolling past terraced rice fields and tea plantations snuggled in the contours of the mountains. I had arrived back at Jakarta's central train station just the night before, tired and achy, desperate for a calming ride on the beauty express.

Oli, inquiring if I would like a shoulder massage, jolts me back to Jakarta. The color was combed into my hair, and there was time for a massage, but did I have enough cash? I calculate: 180,000 *rupiah* for the color, 70,000 for a cut, 90,000 for the combined manicure and pedicure, or about $18, $7, and $9 so far. Guessing the cost of the blow-dry and making sure there would be at least 30,000 left for the cab, I let the ache in my shoulders beat out the butterflies in my stomach and nod OK. Oli deftly takes my arms out of my top and ties the sleeves across my chest. She's done this many times before.

As Oli's hands glide across my shoulders, I realize that I've been skating across the surface of Jakarta like a water bug hovering on the surface of a puddle. Neither exactly expat nor tourist, I take cabs hither and yon, but have no idea who lives and works in the buildings I'm passing, what the teenagers who hang at Blok M are thinking, who shops at the night market, or what beliefs differentiate the women in Muslim dress from their companions in T-shirts and jeans.

The salon's teal-framed windows reveal a Jakarta that stretches out forever, home to more than 12 million people. Inside, I notice my neighbor reading an English-language scandal sheet as her 'do is finished and speculate about where she might be going with her elaborate "*Ibu*" (madam) hairdo—a teased bouffant that bespeaks status and importance. Maybe she's headed to the American ambassador's farewell party, to a congratulatory event for the new Indonesian president, or to one of Indonesia's infamous grand weddings. The real life of Indonesians in Jakarta remains a mystery to me.

Meanwhile, Oli has turned my tired muscles into hamburger, and I'm beginning to overheat from the massage. Perhaps there is such a thing as too much pampering. Hot and suddenly restless, I start to fret about my haircut. Will Sumi get it right? I don't want to come out of the salon with the same orang-locks I brought in. Nor do I want to look as shorn as the short-haired tropical cats stalking the hotel gardens.

Now it's time for The Conversation. Sumi speaks enough English to give me some confidence; she's certainly easier to understand than the Vietnamese manicurists at home in San Francisco. "Okay," I say, "I like the top curly and the back well-shaped. The hard part is just behind my ears where it gets dreadfully thick." Was I too direct? Not clear enough? I hate being so direct in Indonesia, which is known for its culture of indirection. In business, hours are spent socializing before one gets to the point. Even traffic patterns are designed with enormous circular detours that take you blocks, even neighborhoods, out of the way before you can reach your destination.

Sumi starts at the crown of my head; Kathy, my San Francisco stylist, starts at the back of my neck. Sumi cuts in horizontal sections; Kathy uses vertical ones. Despite Oli's hard work, my shoulders tighten and my tummy flops. "Ah, you want me to do layers?" Sumi asks. Do I have to direct every snip? I usually have my nose in *Vogue*, and don't really have a clue. "How about a little more behind my ears? OK, that's good." I finally start to breathe again. This is going to be all right.

In the meantime, Sumi wants to know whether I want a blow-dry. Do I have enough cash? This time we get up and go to the reception desk to look at the bill. With the blow-dry, I have just enough *rupiah* left for tips and a cab back. I sit down again and Sumi takes a small brush to the hair near my ears, pulling it tight and back until it frames my face. The back hugs the nape of my neck, and the top curls softly. The color is a fine rich brunette.

Two hours and five attendants later, the orangutan has finally been tamed. Refreshed and relieved, I settle into the cab for the ride back, relishing each view of the streets around me. In Jakarta, even something as mundane as a haircut is an adventure to savor.

ACCORDION DREAMS

Terri Hinte

I'D BEEN IN MARIENBAD only a day or two, but I understood the lay of the land: the wedding-cake spa house adorned one end of Skalník Park, and the jewel-box Gogol Theater lay near its other end, tucked away on a quiet street. I sat each night in the blue and gold theater, luxuriating in piano recitals given as part of the annual Chopin Festival. By day I'd gaze from afar at the spa house, the temple of secret ablutions.

Curiosity finally won out, and I made plans to remain in Marienbad after the festival to take a spa cure. My days would center around the town's famed waters: imbibing a liter daily from the Forest Spring and immersing myself in marble pools and metal tubs while receiving the ministrations of women in white.

In the wake of the Chopin Festival, Marienbad's nightlife largely evaporated. A mere 15 thousand people resided in the town, which was set in the mountainous forests of western Bohemia. Judging by fliers and posters I saw during my afternoon walks, the Gogol Theater, located just a few steps from my hotel, was the only place to be in the evening hours. Its calendar promised a play by Václav Havel, an appearance by a touring opera company, a concert by an accordion duo named Milan Bláha and Věra. . . Where do I buy a ticket?!

Blaha is my mother's maiden name, and the previous year she and I had come to the Czech lands on a rambling genealogical quest. We found the house where my great-grandfather Václav was born; living in it was a Bláha cousin my mother's age who'd inherited it from his grandfather—my great-great-uncle.

In America, Blaha lost its accent on the "a" but never its foreignness—nor, for me, its fascination. Early on I acquired the habit of looking it up in telephone directories, passing the populous Adamses, Andersons, and Bakers to see if I could unearth a small clump of Blaha people. In the New York City phone books, most of those listed are family to me; in San Francisco, there are none.

When my mother and I, in our travels, consulted the Prague directory, we were astonished to discover 56 Václav Bláhas! A subtle shift occurred in us; a sense of at-homeness took root, even as we battled the language barrier. (I'd spent a year studying my great-grandparents' language in preparation for this trip, and found it a brutal taskmaster, but traveling to the old country without it was unthinkable.)

In the course of our Czech travels Mother and I spent two days in Marienbad, and I became enchanted with its storybook pastel architecture and bucolic setting. As soon as we drove away, in fact, I was missing it, and plotting my return.

Now I found myself at Infocentrum, Marienbad's ticket agency/tourist center, asking the young man on duty for a ticket to Milan Bláha's concert. He could barely contain his surprise at this request. A week earlier he'd sold me Chopin tickets, a far more typical purchase for foreign visitors.

It so happens that I have a sentimental thing for accordions: their bright, wheezing sound takes me right back to my grandparents' Long Island living room, where together we'd watch the Lawrence Welk show every week. My German-speaking grandparents, our upstairs neighbors throughout my childhood, were loyal Welk fans; so were my maternal grandparents, the Blahas. Myron Floren, TV's top accordionist, was a Welk star, and his numbers on the show emphasized the ungainly instrument's traditional oom-pah tendencies or its incipient hokeyness, rather than the sinuous melancholy of the smaller Argentine *bandoneón*, whose acquaintance I was to make years later in San Francisco. Exuberant polkas, not sensuous, dangerous tangos, prevailed in Welk's world.

Now I was about to enter Milan and Věra's world. The concert took place on an unusually warm August evening in the Gogol, a hundred-year-old theater with poor ventilation. This is what people really smell like, I thought, half-choking. But the beauty of the theater, with its two small wraparound balconies and ornate rotunda, compensated somewhat for my discomfort. I sat expectantly in the middle of row seven as the Gogol filled to near-capacity, about 400 souls in search of entertainment. A single folding chair stood in center stage while stage left was cluttered with a bank of speakers and a maze of wires, a second folding chair alongside. Then it was showtime. Milan Bláha emerged from the curtains at the right side of the stage, Věra Ublová from the left, and the pair took their bows with a practiced ease. Milan's droll stage manner proved a perfect foil for flamboyant, dark-haired Věra, a big, fortyish country girl who, over the next 90 minutes, beamed her megawatt smile to the last row of the balconies.

Disappointment set in as I scanned Milan's face for familiar contours. The only possible resemblance was his shiny round pate and narrow fringe of gray hair, a trait handed down by my great-grandfather to each of his male descendants. Unlike my athletic grandfather and his brothers, six-footers all, Milan was short and stocky, more akin to Mikhail Gorbachev and Ed Asner. The boxy, bulky accordion suited his proportions.

The show got underway with chatter. Milan was our genial emcee, greeting the audience first in Czech, then German, then Russian. During each language segment, he asked for applause to determine exactly who was present. Czechs made up the largest group, with a fair number of Germans and a smattering of Russians. "Any others?" he inquired in Czech, almost as an afterthought. This sent me into a panic, an adrenaline attack. I was obviously the only American, in fact the only non-Czech/German/Russian. What if his attempts at English on my account became his whole shtick for the show? Travel for me has always been about having enough language to get into situations where I'm in way over my head, where the ground opens up and swallows me, and occasionally magic unfolds. But here I made a decision to chicken out. Lacking the fluency to riposte with Milan all night or the fortitude to submit to his incomprehensible jokes, I remained the silent observer.

Věra was a born performer who'd be well advised to get her own TV show, and right away. While seated she thrashed about—an aerobic, erotic exercise, every gesture magnified like a stage actress's. Standing, she pounded and pumped her leg to the rhythm with the melodrama of a stadium rock act's lead guitarist.

She used the accordion, which was strapped onto her chest, as an extension of her bosom, heaving it as she played or talked or even breathed, a sort of outrageous punctuation.

Milan, meanwhile, stood or sat placidly and managed to get the job done without veering more than ten degrees to the left or right. Before each song, he'd put on his glasses and turn to the amps and gizmos, studiously plugging and unplugging cords while performing his emcee chores.

The versatile pair's program ranged from Rimsky-Korsakoff to Scott Joplin, polkas to Pink Floyd, and culminated in half a dozen heartfelt encores. Věra Ublová, who'd made a vibrant connection with her audience, seemed to have a hard time saying goodbye.

A couple of days after seeing Milan and Věra, I came across a flier for yet another accordion concert, this one to be held at the beautiful 19th-century Colonnade in the park, midway between the spa house and the Gogol. It was billed as a *Velký Akordeonový Orchestr* (big accordion orchestra), a fitting counterpoint to the duo.

Indeed, the orchestra contained 25 accordionists, all teenagers, plus a trap drummer and even a conga player! Some songs also featured a singer and a three-man trumpet section. Adding to the razzle-dazzle was a squad of baton twirlers who wore a different skimpy outfit for each number. Parents and other family members milled near the Colonnade stage and waited for any chance to applaud adoringly.

My expectations for the *velký* accordion concert were perhaps excessive: an hour of passionate polkas that would set the town spinning. If two accordions could generate *x* amount of excitement, then mightn't 25 produce at least ten times as much? But the music never caught fire. The arrangements were pallid: two dozen accordions playing the same parts resulted in pure monotony. Věra had more juice in her little finger than these players could muster with all their earnest droning. Having experienced her tour de force, I couldn't sit still for this bloodless spectacle.

Instead, I made my way to the spa house for a *minerální koupel*, or mineral bath, and was directed to a ground-floor room facing the park. Two dark metal tubs, tapered and deep, stood at opposite walls; a low-lying upholstered table covered with a white blanket was the room's centerpiece. The attendant, an elfin young woman in white, was filling a tub with fresh bubbling water. She pointed at me, and at the tub, then left me alone in the room.

Gingerly, I stepped into the antique tub and sat down in the tepid water. Pinpoint bubbles massed on my skin, crackling, popping. The water was alive. But for all its explosive fizziness, it felt velvety, soothing. I sank back in bliss.

The attendant appeared at the door to check on me. *"V pořádku?"* she asked sweetly. Everything in order? *"Samozřemě,"* I replied. Absolutely!

After 15 minutes or so, she returned to get me out of the tub and onto the table, over which she'd draped a large white cloth. As she wrapped it around me, shroudlike, the cloth felt crisp, but it softened against the dampness of my skin. Next, she brought the white blanket up and around my swaddled body; a white towel was wrapped around my head and neck. Finally, she placed a folded saffron-colored blanket on top of me. I was safe and serene, cradled.

As the weight of the blankets pressed down on me, I felt myself becoming lighter. A tangle of thoughts dislodged itself and rose up for review: Bláhas, accordions, Václav Havel, Myron Floren. The goulash and *knedliky* I'd eaten for dinner the night before. A couple of secrets I'd harbored for years. All drifted away in the bath house vapors.

The elfin girl came back after a spell and gently removed the saffron blanket. She folded back the white cloth, exposing my foot and shin, and left the room again. Time to stir. I sat up slowly, patting myself with the comforting cloth.

I dressed and walked out of the spa house, floating across Skalník Park, past the Gogol, into the rustling woods at the edge of town. Rose-porcelain sipping cup in hand, I was heading for the Forest Spring to take my afternoon potion, its source deep in the Bohemian earth.

THE TRAVELING GRANNIES

Jeanne Halpern

IF WE HADN'T TAKEN OUR FIRST TRIP on Graduation Day half a century ago and continued to visit each other across the hemisphere and the decades, my life would feel so much more lonely, so much less connected, like an ensemble violinist without her ensemble. And we would not, of course, have become the Grannies, who travel the world together, at least parts of it, every year and a half.

Every day, the photos on my refrigerator door remind me of our adventures. Here, we pose on the deck of a small fishing boat among the islands of the Los Roques Archipelago, just off the coast of Venezuela. We beam under our sun hats, happy, never dreaming that the pilot of the small plane scheduled to pick us up will take a bribe from three rich travelers and fly them back to the mainland instead of us.

Or here we sit, all sisterly in blue jackets, deep underground in a New York City subway station. We wait for a train to Queens to visit the exquisite Isamu Naguchi Garden Museum, where we'll enjoy even the cool raindrops splashing in sculpture pools and on our faces.

And here we stand, arms around each other, laughing, on the last night of our last trip, to Costa Rica, wearing our Jungle Granny baseball caps and our brand-new chartreuse and white T-shirts from La Selva Biological Station. On this trip we exchanged roommates at every stop and feasted our eyes and ears on birds—caracara, scarlet macaws, wood nymphs, trogons—identifying and meticulously recording them. Now I realize that this may be the trip we'll remember longest, in fine-grain detail.

The history of the Traveling Grannies dates back to Graduation Day at Elmira College in June 1956, when Miss Agnes Orbison, our ornithology teacher, gave us her gift.

"There is one area," she said in her authoritative, brought-up-in-India British dialect, waving her hand vaguely toward the southwest, "that you've never seen. I've only been there once, years ago." She gazed off into the distance as though listening to the flutes and chimes of Shangri-La. "A swamp. Yes, the swamp will be my gift to you."

"A swamp?" I asked.

"Yes. You're the only seniors in my freshman class. You've shown such enthusiasm!" And no wonder. The four of us had reached the middle of our senior year, only to discover that we each lacked three of the science credits required for graduation.

And so Pat, Hilary, Emily, and I—against our better judgment and with a touch of guilt for not having breakfast with our parents or packing our suitcases—piled into Miss Orbison's wood-sided station wagon at 5 a.m. on Graduation Day. Though sleepy-eyed, we looked prepared; field guides poked out of our pockets and binoculars bobbed around our necks.

"Not to worry," Miss Orbison assured us, rearranging her telescope and tripod and umbrellas and a large cooler in the back and handing us a can of acrid bug spray. "I'll return you in plenty of time. And I've packed us a picnic breakfast!"

It could be that Hilary, Pat, and Emily believed all would be well, but for me, soon to receive a degree in English literature, Tennyson's "Charge of the Light Brigade" flashed before my eyes: I saw the bold commander lead his troops, trumpets blaring and Union Jacks flying, into disaster.

We did, eventually, stumble on the misty swamp. And yes, we were enthralled by the water birds and also three kinds of woodpeckers rat-tat-tat-tatting from every direction. But we didn't spot the spectacular red-crested pileated woodpecker that had been the subject of my research paper for the course. Finding a pileated had become my dream and my obsession, but we neither discovered its large oval hole in a dead tree trunk nor heard its loud *kuk-kuk-kukuk* echo through the woods. All of us except Miss Orbison got drenched and dirty.

As for graduation, we barely had time to wash and powder our feet so we could squeeze them into high-heeled pumps, safety-pin our gowns so our wet, rolled-up jeans didn't show, and cover our dank hair with mortar boards before walking across the stage to accept awards and diplomas. Nowadays, they'd call this a bonding experience. Back then, it felt like mistake #1 on the road to adult life. Shared mistake #1.

We embarked on our first trip a month or so after graduation, before we went our separate ways—Pat to graduate school in Baltimore to learn to be a teacher, Hilary to Europe on a motor-cycle trip with her sister, and Emily and I to look for jobs in New York City. We set out for Boothbay Harbor, Maine, to visit a college professor, Jean Parker, who had invited us to eat fresh-caught lobster and swordfish straight from the grill in her family's backyard.

"Stop. Back up," Hilary said to me, as I drove my parents' new car for the first time. Her voice betrayed no panic. "You're going up the offramp."

"Hardly any traffic, nobody's exiting," Emily said from the passenger seat, quietly but with certainty. Emily, I thought, is so confident, she should be driving, and I would have offered her the wheel except for my father's warning about insurance coverage. "I'll watch," she said. "You back up."

"Oh, my God," I muttered, eyes fastened on the rearview mirror. My cheeks felt hot and red. With sweaty palms, I shifted into reverse, turned the wheel gradually to the left, then swung the car around. Inside, I was shaking, every act a struggle, but my eyes, hands, and feet kept driving.

"OK," said Pat in her calm voice from behind me, her head slightly out of the window, "straight ahead. See the arrow for Boston?" Her hand lay lightly on my shoulder, a comforting touch.

Thus began our first adventure—brand-new college graduates, in my parents' brand-new white Mercury sedan, on President Eisenhower's brand-new interstate highway system on a drive from Albany to Boston to Boothbay Harbor, Maine. Our first post-college foray into the world, and I could have killed all four of us.

And then came the decades of careers, husbands, children, and grandchildren. After graduate school, Pat found a teaching job in Berkeley, and, even more significantly, she found Norman. They recently celebrated their 46th Christmas-Chanukah together by taking their two grandsons to the Cirque du Soleil. Emily lived in Rome, traveled around Europe, then returned to New York. There she married David, worked in the computer industry, and raised a stepson, a son, and a daughter; now she also has two grandchildren.

Hilary spent several years driving south along the Pan American Highway as it was being built through Central America and then continuing to Tierra del Fuego. She worked as an editor and travel writer in Caracas, Venezuela, where she married Douglas, and had one son and now two grandchildren.

I'd left New York to marry a professor at the University of Michigan, but when our children were eight and nine, my husband died. Even during the difficult years of being a single mom, working and finishing my Ph.D., I stayed in close touch with my three dear friends.

Not long ago, on a warm spring afternoon as Emily and I sat over coffee and biscotti at a parkside café, she said, "I think you kept us connected over all these years—between our first trip together and becoming the Grannies. You were the hub of the wheel. Your spokes reached out to each of us."

"It wasn't just me," I responded, dipping my biscotto a second too long in my cup and watching it disintegrate, except for the top, which I crunched between my teeth.

"Oh yes, it was," she insisted. "I'd always wanted to get to know Pat better, and Hilary—but you visited Pat in California, even before you moved there. And you made those trips to Venezuela to see Hilary—five, six? And at least a dozen to see me in New York."

"Well, I do love free room and board," I laughed. "But really, it was all of us."

"No, Jeanne," she said, with that ring of certainty that brooked no argument. "It wasn't all of us. It was you."

Perhaps because I'm an only child who never really had a "best friend" growing up, I imagine the Grannies' trips mean more to me than they do to the other three Grannies who all have siblings. Being with them has added such intimacy to my life, such a feeling of belonging, such pleasure in being together and creating a history, it is hard to imagine life without our shared adventures. Sometimes I wonder if other women also treasure outings with the same good companions year after year. But I think it must be easier to bake a perfect soufflé than to find three other people—different as they may be in careers, hobbies, choice of husbands, or even using or not using makeup—whose personalities and interests mesh so perfectly. Wherever we go, far away or close to home, we feel satisfied, even joyous being together.

It's not the travel itself that makes our trips special. Each of us has traveled many places in the world, with and without our husbands, children, or friends.

But the bond that has grown among the Grannies during more than half a century has made travel so much easier, so much more comforting, despite the individual catastrophes that may befall us. When I was diagnosed with lymphoma ten years ago, I felt edgy about everything. I was so churned up inside, I left work on short-term disability. I convinced myself not to go on the next Grannies trip, bound for Venezuela. For part of the time, we'd be flown into an isolated area and sleeping in hammocks. I felt, "Oh, what a place to die!" But my oncologist had no such qualms, and the Grannies wouldn't hear of my not going. Was I difficult? Short-tempered? Self-centered? If so, my friends never mentioned it, and I never felt that I was. Nor did I feel favored for my "condition"; I washed dishes like everybody else.

Strangely enough, the four of us were destined to experience much more together than our travels over the years, much more than we ever wanted. Pat was treated for breast cancer, Emily was diagnosed with leukemia. Most recently, Hilary developed very aggressive uterine cancer. Our next Grannies trip was to have been to our 50th Elmira College reunion, with a week or two afterwards in Toronto. Certain that after her surgery and chemo Hilary would recover, we'd even made our hotel reservations— two rooms with two beds each. Were we fooling ourselves into believing the Grannies could come through anything?

Over the years I've often felt that not having another Grannies trip to plan and enjoy would make me feel less whole, less well. And now the uncertainty about our future plans together makes me feel as if I may be losing a part of myself. Yet just as I hold on to the wistful hope that somewhere, sometime, I'll finally find my pileated woodpecker, I now hold on to the deeper hope that the Grannies will, over the years, continue to find joy in each other's company.

TREE SKIN

Kerry Messer

THE FIRST MORNING I stayed at my friend Wai Fun's small flat on the 32nd story of a blocky white government building in Tai Po, I listened to roosters crow, wild dogs bark, and the horns of taxicab drivers down below. Tai Po was built on reclaimed ancient rice paddy fields—all part of a development strategy for the New Territories south of Hong Kong. The hills were covered with jungle-like vegetation accented with white ginger flowers and purple morning glories. The town is home to half a million people.

I saw no rice paddies from Wai Fun's window, but there were old shacks on the hillside overrun by vines, and with squinted eyes I saw figures walking up the steep dirt footpaths.

As I sat in her chair by the window, I noticed a small piece of birch bark the length of my palm and extended fingers. The bark, propped between her computer monitor and keyboard, was the skin of a birch I had given her two years earlier.

Birch is one of those trees that cannot hold onto its skin; like a snake it sheds as it grows. Birch has dirty-snow-on-the-highway bark that sloughs off to expose a paler version of the same tree skin underneath. When I was a kid, I used to pull curling bark from the birch trees near my father's home in New England.

I met Wai Fun many years after I stopped peeling skin from birch trees. She and I worked together in Hong Kong. From the moment we met, we were friends. We shared stories from our childhoods as we sipped jasmine tea in the mornings and noodle soup late in the evenings. We discovered that we both loved nature.

One Sunday we drove out of the city to the New Territories and explored a walled village. I took pictures of water buffalo that stood in mud on their day off from work in the rice paddies. We listened to the clack of mah-jongg pieces on tabletops and the laughter of old men and women playing the game behind partially closed doors.

Wai Fun brought me to a very special banyan tree that she

called the tree house. The tree was ancient and had grown over an old mud-brick house. Almost all signs of the original construction materials were gone, but you could tell a house had been there because the roots of the tree continued to hold the shape of the house that once existed. I took pictures, and Wai Fun smiled. At the end of that day we drove to Victoria Peak in Hong Kong and walked the trail that offered a 360-degree view of the harbor, land, and sea. The air was warm and humid, the waterfalls splashed us, and I told Wai Fun about Vermont, where I spent summers when I was young.

"I have never been to Vermont," she said.

"One day I'll take you, and we'll stand on the bridge my family built over the creek where you'll feel the mountain breeze and hear the water rush beneath your feet."

Our friendship continued to grow, even after our lives moved on from the company that brought us together, and Wai Fun came to visit me. We drove to Vermont from Boston and stayed in my family's old farmhouse. We stood on the bridge over the creek without speaking. Wai Fun cried. I cried too.

We spent the next few days driving around the countryside. Dairy cows salt-and-peppered the green pasturelands, and acres of hay fields and corn offered scenes Wai Fun had only read about or seen in picture books. We drove into the Green Mountains and wound our way up mountain gaps, stopping to walk deep into the woods at secret places with wild waterfalls.

On our last day in Vermont we navigated rutted dirt roads to my favorite tree grove, arriving just as the low-setting sun created a warm, yellow glow that lit the trees.

"What is that?" Wai Fun asked, sitting up in her seat.

"Those are birch trees."

"Birch trees. Birch trees." Wai Fun repeated the words, committing them to memory. "They are beautiful. But actually I wanted to know what is on the ground near the trees."

"That's birch bark."

"I'm sorry, I don't understand what you mean."

"OK. The bark . . . is the tree's skin."

"Oh. I see."

"As the trees grow older each year, the outside layer of the bark peels off."

Wai Fun's eyes grew wide with understanding.

"We have peeling trees in the New Territories, but they are not exactly the same as these." She nodded her head, admiring the white birches that grow in clusters of two, three, and four.

"Can we pick the bark up?" she asked.

"Sure."

I pulled off the road and stopped the car. Wai Fun was worried we were trespassing and might get in trouble for tree-skin poaching. She stayed in the car while I climbed the hillside to collect samples. I ran from tree trunk to tree trunk, trying to conceal my activities. I looked back at the car where Wai Fun sat shaking her head ever so slightly as the daylight faded.

I returned with a stack of the white tree skin in hand.

"I just wanted to look at one piece," Wai Fun said. "We can put the rest back. Tree skin belongs in the woods."

"It's OK; no one will care."

I stacked the pile of bark in the back seat and brought a small, flattened piece to the front seat with me. I handed it to Wai Fun, and she held it to her nose.

"It smells like moss and dirt and looks like sheets of old music."

"Yes, I guess it does." I had never thought to appreciate the smell of the bark. Already Wai Fun knew more than I did about birch bark.

I kept the birch bark peels long after Wai Fun returned to Hong Kong. The bark grew dry and brittle with time, and every time I saw it in my garage I thought of my friend. Finally I laid the curled tree skin on the ground at the foot of a thick pine tree in the woods behind my house.

Wai Fun was right; the bark belonged to the woods. Except for the one small piece I mailed to her with a message written in black ink: "I love you. I'll never forget you, Vermont, and the smell of tree skin."

COMING TO AMERICA

Rina Alcalay

AS MY PLANE LANDED in San Francisco, I brushed my hair and looked out the window, unable to control a yawn of exhaustion. Finally, 22 hours after my flight had left Santiago, I was arriving at my final destination. Butterflies in my stomach, I saw a well-dressed, middle-aged woman waiting for me, carrying a banner with my name. Surprised at this impersonal yet hospitable welcome, I approached her with a smile. She informed me that she was a Stanford International House volunteer who had come to drive me to the University where I would soon be starting a Ph.D. program in Communication. I was 26 years old and had been a professor of Communication Arts at the Catholic University in Santiago. Stanford had offered me a generous scholarship to pursue graduate studies, and the prospect of becoming a student again was exhilarating.

I stared at the highway from her car, taking in the unfamiliar sights. Huge highways, fast cars, tall buildings. It was a sunny September morning and I felt strange, as if I had landed on a foreign planet. The thought that this would be my new home, at least for the next couple of years, started sinking in. I felt uncomfortable, uneasy. Why was I here, what was the point, what had gotten into me that made me leave behind my beloved world, my wonderful friends and colleagues, so many of whom had come the night before to the Santiago airport to bid me farewell?

We got off the highway at a Palo Alto exit and drove through tree-lined streets, into the driveway of a one-story house. "I hope you don't mind stopping at my house for a few minutes," she asked.

"Not at all," said I, not knowing where I was supposed to be going anyway. She asked me to wait for her in the kitchen, which looked on to a back patio with a pool. "What a messy room," I thought. "So dusty and cluttered." So different from the houses I'd left behind. Suddenly, from one of the doors, a sleepy-eyed, bare-chested, teenage boy appeared.

"Hi," he mumbled, as he proceeded to mix eggs and milk in a bowl. He then dipped slices of bread into this mixture, and placed them in a frying pan. "What is he doing?" I wondered, never before having seen the concoction I'd later learn was French toast.

Soon my hostess appeared again, and after a quick goodbye to the young man, obviously her son, we got into her car. A few minutes later, we entered what looked to me like a Spanish hacienda—Stanford University. It was still deserted on that Sunday morning, and classes wouldn't start for another two weeks.

My hostess dropped me at my temporary dormitory, and I entered, my lone suitcase in hand. An athletic-looking young man sat with his feet over a metal desk, busily chewing gum and watching television. He was the only human around, and got up when he saw me. He was in charge of "receiving" the new students. After I gave him my name, he took a set of sheets and a blanket from a metal closet and showed me to my room, on the second floor. I eyed the two bare mattresses, steel table and closet, naked walls, and thick coating of dust over the furniture. I put down the bedding, looked out the window, and collapsed, sobbing, on top of a bed.

I decided that I had made a huge mistake coming to this country, and that I had to go back home instantly. But how would I explain my sudden return to everybody, after all the farewell parties, after all the tears and the many arguments with friends who tried to convince me not to go to the United States in the first place? I would live here for a week, I thought, but only for a week. I would take a plane the following Saturday, and soon this experience would be completely forgotten.

After making this decision I found the bathroom, washed my face, and returned to my room. I felt a pang of hunger, and realized it had been many hours since my last meal. But I knew I'd rather starve than wander outside. Anyway, where would I go, what words would I choose to communicate, would people understand me, would I understand them? I had not used English since high school. Spanish and French had been my personal and professional languages for years. I wiped the dust off the desk, sat down, and started writing a long letter to my parents, explaining the reasons why my coming to the United States had been a colossal mistake.

Halfway through the letter, I heard two knocks at my door and a voice asking: "Would you like to join us for dinner? We are going to the student union for a bite." Intrigued, I opened the door, and two young women were there, smiling. "Hi. I'm Marcia." "And I'm Lindsey," said the other. "We just arrived on campus a couple of hours ago and are going to grab something to eat." "We were wondering if you would like to join us," added Marcia.

"How did they find out I was here?" I thought, pleasantly surprised. They seemed so friendly, and I understood them with no difficulty. Grateful for their kindness, I rapidly answered "Yes," grabbed my purse, and dashed out the door.

Walking along the trails, surrounded by lawns, trees, flowers, and squirrels—I had never seen a squirrel before except in cartoons and in children's books—I started to relax. "So this is what a campus looks like," I thought to myself. It reminded me of a country club. I watched bikers passing us, tennis courts, students sunbathing on the lawns. In Santiago we did not have this separation; universities are part of downtown, and my friends and I would just cross the busy street to eat at a café. There was something unreal about this environment.

We bought our food from one of the several food stations at the student union, took our trays outside, and sat at a table on the terrace. We devoured our supper as we exchanged life stories, surrounded by bluebirds and the sound of a fountain a few steps away.

The day before I had left a Chile long paralyzed by strikes, food scarcity, and political violence. It was the third year of Allende's Marxist regime, and things had gone terribly wrong. For the last few months all commerce was closed, and walking on the streets was risky. I had gotten used to walking close to the buildings, watching for the next portal, ready to jump inside at the first sounds of shots of tear gas and people running down the streets, screaming. Our meetings at work had to be moved to a back room to avoid the random stones coming in from street violence, shattering the front conference room windows. People from all walks of life were desperately trying to find food to feed their families, standing in endless lines to get the essentials. Hatred and distrust among the right and the left had escalated to the point where there was no communication, even among members of the same families.

"Maybe I will give Stanford a month's try instead of a week," I thought as I strolled with my two new friends through the campus back to our temporary dorms, listening to the crickets, talking and laughing in this foreign language, noticing the soft light of dusk embracing the campus buildings, on this, my first day in a new land.

Two days later, on Tuesday morning of September 11, 1973, a violent military coup took over power in Chile, and all communication with my country was interrupted for weeks. I then knew there was no going back. I had better embrace what was to become my new home.

THE WRITING LIFE

LOCATING MEMORY, LOCATING SELF

Trena Noval

ON A VISIT to my 92-year-old friend Lorna, I shuffled through piles of manila folders searching for one that she said simply had the word "Paris" written on it.

"Is it this one?" I asked her.

She stared at me anxiously. "No. Keep looking."

After a few moments, I saw the word scrawled across a folder tab. I studied the writing for a few seconds. Paris. The single word denoted volumes of moments, a life's worth. The word was written with a shaky hand. Lorna has not been able to write for the last few years, and I wondered when she made this file.

"Now find the yellow-lined paper in there and read me what it says."

The page was handwritten, but some years ago. The writing was clear and steady.

I began:

"The smell of the brisk autumn air, the lights in the streets, the people passing over the bridge, walking in the wind, it feels good. The bookseller waves to me. I keep looking for Felo in the street, to come walking up to me, home from his day. I see him coming down the street, see his hat and then his face smiling at me under the streetlight. He has pages of sheet music rolled under his arm. It is starting to snow very lightly. I smile back, and he slips his warm hand in mine and we melt into one. We walk together in the night down a street in Paris. . . "

I read it again to her, this time more slowly. She closed her eyes the whole time, humming low and softly. She had drifted off into another world.

When I finished reading, she stayed in that place, eyes closed, humming. After a while, she opened her eyes with a smile, as if it were the first moment after a kiss, so tender and gentle leaving her lips. She wheeled her chair over to me sitting on the side of her bed with the folder in my lap and took the sheet from my hand. She studied it even though she could no longer read the words and dropped her head into her hands.

"That's what happens when you get old, when you have lived as long as I have. You get all these memories that keep you going, keep you living. They just come and go. I can't control them."

Although much younger, I knew what she meant; I have had those desperate urges to recall a moment, trying to shape a story, recall a detail that was so important, looking for a piece of who I was.

My son Sam came home from school one day in the third grade with a homework assignment to bring in pictures from his life, from times that were important and people that meant something to him. He was going to create his first autobiography. Such a daunting task this was for us, so many boxes of pictures, not clearly marked with years or places. It was like taking a journey, a long winding one. Not only for Sam, but for me, watching the events of the last nine years of life unfold, the good and the bad. I could barely tear myself away to help Sam, getting caught up in my own world of memories.

There were pictures of me in different versions of haircuts, the various stages of my parents aging though time, and all the images of Sam in babyhood. I started to feel a lump well up in my throat—I realized that something had happened to me that I thought never would: I had drifted so far away from those moments that I couldn't remember what they felt like. Sam's soft baby skin, the feel of small arms around my neck, grabbing his little fat legs as he crawled on the floor under the table. Then even earlier memories came: the sound of my father's voice singing to me when I was young, the bellowing laughter of my grandmother, and later when I grew up, the passion of my first lover.

I think I must have thought about writing all my life. From very young I was a daydreamer, creating stories in my head. It took many years to get to this point where I have the confidence to put words on a page for others to read. And I am learning to become more polished, learning to better craft my words. Even now as I write, moments from my life drift in and out of focus trying to force their way onto the page, things that I had forgotten or painfully tucked away.

I remember my mother's need to see my father's feet after he died. He lay in their bed of 35 years, his feet snugly tucked in socks because he was so cold all the time near the end. His feet looked like two small mountains under the blankets at the foot of the bed. He had such lovely elegant feet. My mother asked me to fold back the blankets and take his socks off so that she could see his feet, but I couldn't do it for her, and she couldn't do it for herself. None of us in the room could move. I felt as if I just couldn't disturb him, the way he looked, and I was afraid of the weight that his leg and foot would bear if I tried to lift them to remove his sock. I didn't want to feel the weight of his death. I wasn't ready. We just stood there and stared at him frozen in our own time.

Earlier that morning at about 5:00 my sister BJ woke me. She was gently rubbing my back, calmly, lovingly. I heard her whisper to me in my sleeping fog, calling my name. Trena. Dad died in his sleep, she whispered. I sat up and tried to piece it all together— what had happened, what it was like that moment she heard the phone ring, who called to tell us, what they said, how it was delivered. It was still dark and cold. I didn't hear the phone ring, I was dreaming in BJ's queen-size guest bed, with Sam curled up asleep next to me, and my husband James sleeping in the room next door. I only felt the touch of my sister's hand on my back that morning and heard her call my name in a whisper. I knew what it was about when I heard her whisper my name.

BJ and I got up and lingered a long time drinking coffee before we went over to see my father. We knew as long as we sat there at her kitchen table our day would be normal, as if nothing had happened.

Later that morning the undertaker rolled my father's body out of the house on a gurney through the garage door. When Sam showed up with James he poked his head around the corner of my parents' bedroom doorframe several times, trying to figure it all out, the empty bed, the sunlight streaming in, the silence in the room. He was three and a half years old on that day. He just kept looking every so often, but didn't say a word.

James, Sam, and I had temporarily moved back home to New

Jersey when my father became ill. After his death, I thought I could stay on with my mother for a while, help her get settled into her new life without him. But I couldn't stay after the funeral. I couldn't breathe in that house. I was afraid it would suffocate me. I didn't know what to do with my time. I had been consumed for those last three months by taking care of my father. Once that job was done, I didn't understand what my place would be there. So I went home to try to learn to grieve and to let my mother do it in her own way, without the interruption of a daughter and young grandson. She told me she threw her wedding ring across the room and left it there for a few weeks. She was mad. Mad at my father for leaving her, mad that she felt so alone. She wouldn't wear her ring for a few years. She said she wasn't married to my father anymore. But she wears it now. She has learned to feel OK about the memories it holds, I guess.

My grieving has not moved in a big wave like my mother's. Over the past five years it has let itself out in small moments over time. Walking down the street, I recognize the shoes on an older man, the size of them, the color and gait of the walk as he passes by. Or a memory will float into my head while I'm driving my car of a funny phone message my father once left me that made me laugh. Rubbing my son's back at night to lull him to sleep, I remember my father did that with me. Moments I can't control, as Lorna said; they just come and go, briefly throwing me off track.

I know now the reasons why I have taken to writing, finally allowing words to make their way to a page. I write because I want more than a 4x6 snapshot to describe the depth and details of those moments. To remember what they felt like, what they sounded like, those voices and words that spilled out into my life. I write to remember the things that I would never photograph but need to be known. And I write to find that place again and again, to locate the memory of those feelings that I have locked away.

I write to find my self.

FALLOW

Terri Hinte

MY FAVORITE BOOK TITLE OF LATE is Geoff Dyer's *Yoga for People Who Can't Be Bothered to Do It*. It resonates for me because of possible implications not about the vigor of my yoga practice—which chugs along in its fashion—but about my writing practice, which is quite dormant. The well seems to be dry; the pump is assuredly not primed. Nothing's happening.

I'm a longtime "Wednesday Writer," but the writing of mine contained in our first book is old writing, even years old. Lately in-class exercises are all fits and starts—and blanks. Right now nothing's happening.

What I'm much more interested in these days is the ongoing work in my backyard garden—the discovery and selection and arrangement of plants. In the far-right corner, in front of a stucco mural created by a friend, there's a place for a melianthus major, or honey bush, with jagged gray-green leaves and, so I'm told, foot-long spikes of brick-red flowers. Outside one bedroom window, I'll watch a two-foot-tall fuchsia boliviana alba turn into a small tree producing pendulous clusters of scarlet-tipped tubular white flowers.

And towering over everything is the incense cedar, occupying the place of honor in the yard since the 1940s. I was apprehensive about how the new irrigation lines might affect the tree's health, so I called an arborist in for a consultation. A few days later, he and I spent an hour in the yard, talking about the cedar. This required us to crane our necks uncomfortably in order to view the needly canopy 30 feet over our heads. Peter, the arborist, turned out to be a fan of incense cedars, and he found much to admire in this particular specimen. But in light of its age, and the garden work in progress, he had concerns about the "invisible tree"—the root system, which covered an area as wide as the tree was tall, filling my entire yard as well as that of the neighbor behind me. Peter suggested an aeration program, in which he would drill 18-inch holes all over the yard (and my neighbor's) and shoot them full of rich liquid compost. This treatment would enhance the cedar's ability to take in nourishment and increase the likelihood that its remaining 60 to 80 years would be lived out in vibrant health. We would hope to see signs of that health—new growth—after a few seasons.

I, too, await signs of life—signs of something—in my writing. I'm feeding my mind and my soul, and showing up at the page, so it's just a matter of time, isn't it? before the well can be drawn from again. But there's satisfaction, too, in having written. "Dream Job," my four-year-old story about Mr. Franklin, the blind man I was assisting to write his memoirs, has now been published in our book and in the *East Bay Monthly*. I found myself suddenly—and belatedly—moved to realize that this story, which Mr. Franklin had fervently wished to be told, has finally reached its audience. By telling me his story over and over again 30 years ago, he planted a seed that has at last come to fruition on the printed page.

My friend Laurie says that writing is a river, an immense river fed by countless tributaries large and small. Even the most modest piece of writing feeds the river—the same river Doris Lessing finds herself in, or Dostoevsky, or the Wednesday Writers. I'm trying to keep a toe in the water, knowing that at any time now I could get caught up in the current. I could soon be writing again.

THE AWAKENING

Laura Shumaker

I MET TRACY when I moved to the neighborhood five years ago. At the time, I had a lot going on. I was raising three boys, the oldest autistic, and was balancing their care with that of my mother, who was very ill. I was tired and emotionally drained. After Tracy and I traded introductions, she asked me the dreaded question.

"What do you do?"

I could tell by her manner that she didn't really care what *I* did; she just wanted to tell me what *she* did.

I gestured feebly to my three boys jumping around on my front lawn, the eldest stuffing a worm down a drain with a devilish look on his face. Tracy cocked her head and crinkled her brow with a "you poor thing" expression.

Before I could reply with "home with kids, oldest autistic, mother sick," Tracy blurted out, "I'm a writer!"

She was beaming.

After a brief conversation—how many kids, how old, great neighborhood, love to go for a walk sometime—she skipped away, and I wondered, what does she write about? I might like to write, too. God knows I have great material, having been through years of daily adventures trudging through the maze of autism. Then my oldest son, Matthew, bolted impulsively toward the street, and I thought, ruefully, when would I write?

I had always enjoyed writing in a journal as a young girl, but by college had been reduced to knocking out English papers between the hours of midnight and 7 a.m. for my 8:00 class. Writing had become a game, rather than a passion, and the IBM Selectric was stowed away in the hall closet after graduation. I was distracted by the excitement of life in San Francisco with friends, work, and romance, blissfully unaware of what struggles lay ahead.

Years later, when I relayed stories about Matthew, people would say, "You could write a book!" My father urged me to start a journal, and my husband agreed. But every day was a frantic mix of unexpected phone calls from school, neighbors, and eventually law enforcement—all upset by Matthew's disruptive, impulsive behavior. Damage control was my way of life. I delivered flowers to his teacher after a tough day, a bottle of wine to the neighbor who had found Matthew in her yard gleefully throwing basketballs and soccer balls into her swimming pool, and I circulated brochures to police officers about autism to educate them that his strange behavior was not drug-related. In the midst of it all, I managed to make frequent visits to my beloved mother, and nurture, with the help of my supportive husband, my two other sons.

After my mother died, my father started writing. . . beautifully. He wrote about his happy childhood on the Monterey Peninsula in the '30s, the oldest of five, oblivious to the fact that the country was in the midst of the Great Depression. He wrote about his family, a colorful bunch, and his friends—about Valentine's Day in the third grade. He wrote about things he remembered and didn't want to forget. In one story, he is six years old, and his daddy the fireman and forest ranger drives by in a shiny red fire truck, smiling and waving, siren blaring. My father's pride jumped off the page and moved me to tears. Whenever I visited him in Carmel, he couldn't wait for me to sit down in the white chair by the window and read his pieces. He studied my face as I read his stories, waiting for my reaction to the sentence he knew would make me laugh, and teared up when I lifted my eyes from the page to meet his. I noticed the twinkle in his eye, the amused smile on his face. I told him, "You ought to have this published!"

"Just a hobby" was his reply.

It wasn't till the following summer when I felt an urgent need to write. My mother had been gone about a year, and my husband and I had placed Matthew in a special school in Pennsylvania. Friends and family thought I would be relieved when Matthew left, that I would finally get a break. But instead, I felt an emptiness and sorrow too acute to share with anyone, and I needed to write about it.

I started to write stories of my life with Matthew, starting with the wonderful days of his infancy and toddlerhood when we thought he was perfect, through the heartbreak of diagnosis up to the more recent years of survival and acceptance. I wrote of being the mother of an autistic child, and of the discoveries regarding human character, good and bad, that I made along the way. I joined a women writers' group, enrolled in writing workshops at a local independent bookstore, and took extension courses at a nearby college.

Now I take my yellow pad with me everywhere, and turn to it in idle moments. I think—what do people need to know about Matthew? How can I paint a picture of him and of his place in the world? As the ideas wash over me, I jot them down frantically till the one that illustrates him best stares back at me, and I silently rejoice.

I look forward to my writers' group each Wednesday as if it were the first day of school, and when I come home afterward, I am so full of energy that I have to keep moving, usually folding the laundry and cleaning the house that I have neglected in favor of my new friend, the gray laptop. There have been days when my husband and children have had to remind me to feed them dinner, but they smile when they feel my excitement. They are proud of me.

At times, writing unearths dark feelings, long buried, as I remember the moment the psychologist first uttered the word autism, or the haunting questions from insensitive friends. "Will he ever live on his own or hold a job?" On days when I plunge into a well of unbearable sadness, the only way to climb out is by turning to humor. I write funny stories that make me laugh out loud as I work. Some of these stories I share with others, but usually they are just for me. Once I am lifted out of my funk, I dare to share my writing. The thrill of moving family and friends to tears or laughter, crafting the perfect sentence, or seeing my name in print allows me to store the dark days away until I have the courage to revisit them.

While writing about my journey with Matthew has been difficult at times, it has been illuminating. When I recount where we started and all the challenges along the way, I have a newfound appreciation of what a struggle it is to *be* Matthew. It is my job as his mother to help him navigate his way through life within the confines of his disability while steering those in his path toward understanding and acceptance.

Writing has been an awakening, an energizing preoccupation, and now I understand Tracy's eager proclamation and the twinkle in my father's eyes. There is a new dimension in my life, and I see and feel everything with inspired clarity. I am a writer.

THE PERFECT MOMENT

Kate Ruddle

THERE WERE SO MANY perfect moments this week in which to write. This is not one of them. This is the last moment. The moment before it is too late. The moment before I lose my moment. This is Tuesday morning, my usual writing time. If I really am prepared it is Monday, but Monday is usually a day of thoughts interspersed with attempted actions, whereas Tuesday is usually a day where things can happen. Tuesday morning, the day before Wednesday. Hopefully enough time to write and edit and prepare. Why do I wait until Tuesday?

Last Wednesday I took the class journal. Wednesday afternoon seemed the "perfect moment." I was excited after reading my essay to the group. I had tapped into something important, something meaningful. I was charged up about my ideas and about my writing. The support of the group flowed through me. I drove to Lake Merritt and pulled my truck into a spot. I carried my lunch, the group journal, and my notebook to the bubbly, gurgling manmade stream in the park that I like. I suppose it's crafted, but it feels natural, it flows across rocks, and drips down and moves along. Now is the "perfect moment" to write, I thought, as I pulled out the journal. I leafed through it looking at others' handwriting, noticing how someone had pasted in a passage typed on a computer. Am I ready?

Maybe I'll write first in my notebook and transfer it later. I wrote for an hour fully confident that I would go back and edit it later, but I couldn't touch it again before Wednesday. Half of the essay was too close and personal, and the other half developed into a cold, abstract, and analytical tirade on "why feminism failed." It was an essay with two personalities, one that I was not ready to include. It seemed out of place in a journal with so many women's voices.

Thursday night was another "perfect moment." The house

was quiet with my boyfriend away at band practice, and the only sound of drumming was the sound of the rain steadily falling on the roof. It made me feel sleepy and cozy. I thought of the journal. Maybe I'll read some of the other women's essays first, I thought. I had done that the first time I had the journal, and it had been such a pleasure to share in their voices, in their experiences. But somehow I avoided it; it didn't feel right this time, and I dozed instead.

Saturday afternoon felt like another "perfect moment." I was sitting outside under my walnut tree in the yard. I had just finished lunch and was tired from teaching my drawing class. The funny thing about this "perfect moment" was that I was able to notice how it would change from being the "perfect moment," when I was sitting in my chair in the sun, to the "worst possible moment," when I thought of actually getting up and getting the journal and putting pen to paper. In that next moment I was suddenly too tired, too burnt out, afraid that I'd ruin my opportunity to write in the journal by writing something inadequate, by not being up to the task.

So I'd sink back in my chair in the sun and daydream about how, once again, it was the "perfect moment." I ended up going kayaking for the first time by myself. I rented a kayak and headed out onto the smooth water feeling exhausted and perplexed that this thin sheet of glass-like surface was keeping me out of such depths. I returned feeling the strength in my arms powerfully pulling me forward.

Then I began to write.

THE PAGE IN FRONT OF ME

Martha Slavin

AFTER I ACCEPTED the writers' group journal, I froze. Suddenly as I sat staring at the small green book, I began to doubt my ability to face the page. Suddenly the journal grew in proportion to its longevity—more than ten years of writings from many different women. These pages were no longer just a week's worth of jottings. Suddenly I felt that I had to measure up to some standard that had settled itself in the book through the thoughtful writings that filled it. I have ideas circling around in my head, but none of them had drawn more than a sketch of workable beginnings. As I write the first entry for a new session, then, it is appropriate that I just begin with some of those sketches: a letter to the former Pakistani ambassador to France whom I met at a party; teenagers on a bus; whom do I know who is gorgeous; and daffodils resurfacing. None of these beginnings is complete yet; but if I write them down, perhaps they will act like the daffodils and persist.

We have a cluster of daffodils in our front yard. They have been there since 1983 despite the efforts of gophers and rain. They come up every year in January. First, the solid green leaves push away the clay soil; then, the buds shoot up tightly closed; finally, around Presidents' Day in February, the cups open up and turn to the sun. Just as predictably, we have a hard rain that week that smacks the daffodils to the ground, spraying their petals with dirt. For 20 years these daffodils have come up; for 20 years, the rains have been just as persistent. What tenacity the daffodils have. They never quit trying.

A group of rambunctious teenagers scrambled on the Parisian bus, pushing and jostling each other. I steeled myself for the English that I expected to spew from their mouths—another horrid example of Americans in Paris. But to my surprise, they called out to each other in French. They were on the way home from school, their packs slung carelessly on the floor, impeding anyone else's progress to the back of the bus. The bus wasn't too full, just my son and me, a few older men in the back, and a grouping of women of all ages in the front where the boys parked themselves. In the U.S., the boys would continue with their carousing, disturbing everyone's peace without eliciting any reaction. These boys' noisy banter was unusual for French students. In the morning on another bus, quiet teenagers greeted each other with the quick touch of each cheek, but quickly resumed studying their script-filled pages of notes. French schools are rigorous and expect students to memorize what their teachers give them on a routine basis. The bus ride is a time to study.

That afternoon, though, the boys were feeling cocky, exuding their newfound manliness. They showed off to the crowd, who didn't like it one bit. The women on the bus began to give them dagger-stares, affronted that these boys could be so ill-mannered. Finally one woman and then another began to scold the boys, their voices raised in anger until one of the women slapped one boy on the arm. The boys stopped their roughhousing in surprise, sidled to the exit, and jumped off at the next stop.

Dear Mr. Chaudry,
You naturally held the attention of everyone at the dinner table. It was your house, after all; you were an erudite man; and with your sad demeanor, you seemed to carry the whole weight of Pakistan on your shoulder. You questioned why the West criticized countries like Pakistan for their treatment of women. "Isn't my wife a supreme example of the power of women in Pakistan?" you asked. Your wife was also a diplomat, had just completed her Ph.D., and was returning shortly to Pakistan to take a test to further her place in the diplomatic service. How could the West criticize Pakistan when women there could reach such high places? What you didn't mention was that your wife was one of a small number of elite women who profited from educational opportunities, while many women in Pakistan do not.

Oprah's O magazine offered a prize this month for the best story about a friend who was gorgeous. I thought, "Wow, that would be easy to write about a friend." The word "gorgeous" threw me, though. What does gorgeous really mean and would I want to call good friends gorgeous when there are so many better words to describe them? Gorgeous means rich, superb, grand, brilliant, resplendent, glittering, dazzling. I would think such a person would be hard to be with. Perhaps the word "gorgeous," like the word "brilliant" in England, is used more regionally—is this a Chicago word? When I think of my friends, I think of words such as helpful, salt-of-the-earth, quick, intelligent, full of life, good listeners as well as good storytellers, full of adventure and kindness. They are beautiful in spirit as well as looks, but gorgeous isn't a word I would use to describe them.

With this journal in my hand, I imagine the women who belong to the writers' group, and think about all the thoughtful words they have entered here, as well as their submissions to the group in other forms. How we have all grown from listening to all of our voices; how comforting it is to be in such a group. How funny that I would hesitate to write in the journal one more time. I need to look at the daffodils outside my window, and following their example, I need to persist in filling the page in front of me.

8
HEALING WORDS

HOW TO HELP
A STUBBORN SICK FRIEND

Marian Magid

"JUST LET ME KNOW if I can shop or run some errands for you."

I heard that offer again and again when I was housebound with torn ligaments in my foot and various other ailments.

I never did ask those kind folks for help. As a congenitally independent type used to being the one who took care of others, I just couldn't bring myself to call on them. It was more than stubbornness that held me back. I felt a rush of fear every time I contemplated giving up the self-reliance that had served me well for a lifetime.

But some in my circle were caring and creative enough to break through the defenses of a crusty, I'll-do-it-myself type like me.

The first friend who wouldn't take "no" for an answer jumped right in when she saw me limping a few hours after I tripped and twisted my foot.

"I won't let you go through the weekend without seeing a doctor for a foot that looks like that," she announced. She made me an appointment for the next day, which I obediently and gratefully kept.

Once the doctor ordered me to stay off my foot, other friends and relatives found ingenious ways to do end runs around my reluctance to be a "burden."

"Tomorrow I'll be shopping at Costco. Just give me your shopping list," a neighbor virtually demanded. Since I'm really good at taking orders, I immediately gave her a list—and loved getting all my favorite groceries delivered.

My husband was even better at not giving me a chance to object. "I raked the leaves because I know it bothers you not being able to do it yourself" or "I'll be home at two o'clock to take you to the doctor" or "I brought you one of your favorite burgers."

Assertiveness dissolved my resistance every time. "I know

how much you love my brisket," said a gourmet pal. "I'll deliver some tomorrow at five." The brisket turned out to be a tonic for my body and soul, as she somehow knew it would be.

And even I couldn't reject an orthopedist friend's decision to make a house call. "I'm on my way over to teach you some exercises to strengthen your foot once the cast is off." I just said "Thanks," and was so grateful for his help and for offering it in a way I couldn't turn down.

Some friends were more subtle. They tempted me irresistibly to stay in the loop of life. "We need you at the meeting tomorrow, so I'll pick you up and help you navigate the stairs." I was still needed—yay! You can bet I was ready an hour early.

The best barrier-breaker of all was unconditional love. "How are you feeling today? I *really* want to know." My kids just wouldn't accept "fine" for an answer, so when they called or stopped by I *told* them how I felt—at length—and felt so much better each time I did, though I'd never have unburdened myself without their loving and insistent prompts.

What enabled me to override my unreasonable but very real terror of dependence was getting specific gestures of help from people who understood my needs and fulfilled them, without expecting me to ask. Their nonjudgmental acceptance of my personality quirks, their intuition, and their determination to find a way to be there for me even though I didn't make it easy moves me to tears each time I recall their generous acts.

After this experience, I'll never again say to someone like me who's ailing, "Let me know if I can do anything for you." From now on, I'll figure out exactly what would help my dear one heal—and then I'll just *do* it.

STOPPED IN MY TRACKS

Kathleen Faraday

I HAVE BEEN STOPPED in my tracks—literally. Three weeks ago I had foot surgery, and no longer do I jump out of bed at 5:30 a.m. to join my friends for our daily 6 a.m. walk around the Lafayette Reservoir. I was fearful of the surgery and imagined the pounds piling on with each sedentary day. I had trouble thinking about how I would cope.

Today I awoke at 5:30 a.m. as I never reset my alarm. I now welcome the time to lie in bed quietly gathering my thoughts and reviewing my life. I have been slowed down, protected from that other frenetic me who tries to cram as much as is physically possible into a single day.

I have spent hours working at my desk with my foot propped up and wrapped in ice. I have phoned friends who have recovered from similar bunion surgery for reassurance. Then I realized that this has actually been a blessed experience. I took this home-bound opportunity to book the professional organizer who has helped me to clear out clutter. It sounds so simple and to some ridiculous, but I need a real taskmaster to pose the questions: "You need this—why?" "You'll use this—when?"

We have gone through closets, cupboards, storerooms: letters to my deceased husband from his mother, my children's grade-school memorabilia, keepsakes, pictures, and more pictures. Deborah sorted things into categories—memories, to throw away, to recycle. It was emotional, exhausting, and expensive, but, above all, it was freeing. I recently heard someone say, "Stuff hurts." It does. I was reliving my life with each piece of memorabilia— the joys and the pain. I am letting go of the yesterdays with many "could haves" and "should haves." One evening I went through nine years of my newspaper columns and put them in order in plastic sleeves—such a simple task, but I had never taken the time.

The doctor removed the stitches from my foot yesterday and told me to try wearing a regular shoe. I am afraid—fearful that I will press on the accelerator of my life, that I'll revert back to my other self.

I am watching my cat chase a small shiny rock around my office. My other cat just joined in the rock game, and they've chased it under the Mongolian saddle rug. The old me wouldn't have taken this moment.

PORTRAITS

Christy Myers

FLIPPING THROUGH a design magazine, I spied a sumptuously decorated dining room with a painting of a man dressed in a suit, his hand resting on the back of a chair. I imagined a large portrait of my husband Ken in a similar pose with his hand on a chair, since furniture is his business. Thomasville Furniture Company, where Ken worked for 32 years, began as a chair company. In Thomasville, North Carolina, the town that gives the company its name, there is a statue of a giant chair in the center of downtown. Over the years, Ken and his business partner Giles both climbed up and sat in the huge Duncan Phife chair to have their picture taken. The company gives a reproduction of the same chair to the salesman of the year, and both Giles and Ken have received it.

Once I had the idea for the painting, I asked Ken to pose. He arranged himself in his typical salesman stance, wearing a gray pinstriped suit, one hand on the back of his commemorative chair and the other on his hip. After I got the basics down on my canvas, I didn't always need Ken in the room while I worked on the painting. As he passed by my studio on the way to his home office, he'd stop and look at the painting thoughtfully, turning his head one way and then the other, and say, "I think the shoulders should be wider" or "smaller waist" or "more hair."

What really struck me was the closeness I felt with him while I painted his face and his hands. I worked on his mouth slowly with a tiny brush to create the nuances that are Ken, my love. From time to time I stepped back to review my labors. The curve of the mouth wasn't quite right. I'd load my brush with paint and go back at it. I worked the canvas with minute strokes to get the mouth to feel right. He has tiny spaces between his teeth and his eyes are green with a special shine. I was trying to create an image that would capture the distinct personality of this one man who was like none other in this world. Painting is like writing about a loved one, choosing the right words to portray that special individual.

I have painted many portraits, and each time I feel the same. I become intimate with the fine details of the person I'm painting. I've only painted people I know well. I painted my son Bryan when he was about 22. He was becoming a man, as handsome as a young man can be and vulnerable to the world he was about to face. I painted him at that age, with an image of him as a boy and also as a baby superimposed on his chest. It was an image of my boy at different stages of his young life.

The portrait that caught me up in a whirl of emotion was of Giles, Ken's longtime partner. Giles was "one hell of a guy," gregarious, fun, and full of practical jokes, always the life of the party. We could hardly believe him when he told us he would die of prostate cancer before he was even 65. I had a strong desire to paint his portrait before he died. I searched through our photographs of vacations spent with Giles and his wife Jana spanning many years, from Bermuda in spring to the fall colors in Maine. I came up with a composition of Giles leaning casually on his commemorative Thomasville chair. He was wearing a T-shirt designed for the prostate cancer wellness group he helped organize during his four-year illness.

Again I had the same feelings I'd had while painting Ken's portrait, realizing the details that made up the smiling face of our great friend. At times I couldn't stop the tears while I painted Giles, knowing we would lose him soon. His bony arthritic fingers wearing his distinctive gold wedding ring were difficult to capture, but I kept at it. When the painting was finished, I brought it to his house. It was wrapped in brown paper. By this late date Giles was wasting away. Mixed feelings swept through me. I had to paint his portrait because it was a gift I knew I had to share with him and those who knew him, and I had to give it to him before he died so he would know how much I loved him. When I ripped away the paper to reveal the painting of this man in all his living vibrancy, he and Jana spilled tears of happiness and sorrow. Looking at the painting, Giles saw himself full of life. He knew others would see the portrait and remember him as he was. On the corner of the painting I wrote, "Safe Journey Giles, Christy."

MY SEASON IN HELL

Lori Rosenthal

IN DECEMBER 2000, when I crossed the finish line of the 26.2-mile Honolulu Marathon, I was handed a neon-orange finisher's T-shirt and a puka-shell victory necklace. I slipped both over my head with pride and kept walking to keep my legs from cramping up. Despite blistered feet, sore muscles, and sunburn, I felt as if I owned the world. Even though I ached for days, an ear-to-ear grin of achievement stayed plastered to my face for weeks.

Two months later, and back in my everyday routine, I was sitting in the gynecologist's office, waiting to see the doctor. Six months prior, a Pap smear had indicated abnormal cells in my cervix. In a procedure done the month before, those cells had been biopsied. Now they would be removed. I wasn't worried about the procedure. I had a more immediate concern. There was a scant 45 minutes remaining on my parking meter and a high likelihood of getting a ticket. Not a welcome thought. The nurses assured me I would be out of the office within 30 minutes and back at my car before the meter expired. I undressed, sat back, and waited for the gynecologist, while reading a magazine story about the breakup of some trendy Hollywood couple.

The gynecologist came into the room and, after exchanging pleasantries, dropped a verbal bomb that would continue to reverberate to this day. She informed me that my recent lab work came back with an unexpected cancer diagnosis. She told me that we were going ahead with the planned procedure and would use the results to determine where the cancerous cells were.

From that moment on, the room split into two scenes. I was in both of them, as in the movie *Annie Hall*, when Woody Allen is in bed having sex with Diane Keaton, but also sitting in the nearby chair and talking about it. One conversation unfolded completely in my mind about having cancer, deciding who would raise my kids, saying tearful goodbyes, and dying. The other conversation was spoken aloud with the gynecologist. "I have what? You're going to do what? The operation will be when? This is really cancer? What are the next steps? Say that again?" In short, this was not turning out to be a good day.

I assumed "the position," momentarily appreciating the lovely seascape poster on the ceiling. The gynecologist proceeded to do her thing. The procedure hurt. In retrospect I don't know if the pain came from the procedure itself or the word cancer that was echoing throughout my brain. CANCER. Cancer. CaNcEr. YOU HAVE CANCER. Kind of like AOL's "You have mail." Or the voice-mail greeting that says, "You have five new messages." But really, it was completely different. It was more like: "*Lori, you have a big problem. You are in deep shit.*"

After the procedure I got dressed and met the gynecologist in her office. She patiently listed what needed to happen next. I was to get a blood test, a chest X-ray, an abdominal CT test, and meet with the oncologist. With the test results available so far, they both recommended a hysterectomy within the next 60 days as the best way to remove the cancer. Additional information and the advice of specialists, who would be reviewing my test results, might change that recommendation. More or different treatment might be needed. The oncologist and I would make the final call. I left the office in a daze and stumbled to my car.

In the car, with the meter expired and no ticket on the windshield, I sat and cried. I did have the presence of mind to know that I wasn't going back to work that day. On the way home I rented a video, *Keeping the Faith*, and then settled into bed with two things on my mind. One, my abdomen hurt like hell and I needed to get off my feet. Two, I needed to stop thinking about this word, CANCER.

At home, before I turned the video on, I called my husband David and spilled both my guts and bucket-loads of tears. I asked him to call the gynecologist and check that I had heard her correctly. Unfortunately, it turned out that I had been an accurate listener.

I watched the video for a while. Then I got up my strength to schedule the appointments needed to keep this process moving forward. During the next half hour, while on the phone scheduling these appointments, I said the word C-A-N-C-E-R 18 times. I counted. I then watched more of the movie, starting and stopping as my courage mounted to take on new tasks. I called my mother and family members. I called my best friend. I called in to work. By dinner that night, I was able to utter the word CANCER without crying or stumbling. I had come a long way in a few short hours.

Days passed in a depressed blur as I came and went from different doctors' appointments. I kept calling the oncologist's office to move up our initial meeting, but he was waiting to receive my test results and wouldn't schedule an appointment without them. I got more and more anxious with fears that the cancer was spreading all over my body. At times I was sure I could feel it.

I kept up the outer shell of normal life, continued a minimum presence at work, and spent my unscheduled time in bed watching videos. That was my coping mechanism. It kept me from thinking about my situation. And from 2 to 4 a.m., in those sleepless morning hours, I visited cancer sites on the Internet and pursued a virtual Berlitz course in the new and difficult language of oncology. At odd times of day or night I broke out in tears for no apparent reason. (Oh right, cancer. I forgot.) My girlfriends were quite willing to sit and let me cry.

Two weeks after being told I had cancer, I drove with David to the oncologist appointment. The doctor patiently answered my long list of meticulously prepared questions. He explained what would happen from then through the surgery date. My brain turned off halfway through the overview. David kept listening closely and taking detailed notes that I could consult later. That was his appointed task.

The oncologist then examined me. He said he didn't feel anything out of the ordinary that would complicate things, and thought we would be able to remove the cancer cells. The surgery was scheduled for three weeks from that day. I left the appointment with a sense of hopefulness I hadn't had in a while. David and I stopped for Chinese food on the way home. Cancer or no cancer, nothing gets in the way of food in our family.

What does it mean to have cancer? I used to think it meant the kiss of death. With just a few weeks remaining until surgery,

I began to change my perspective. I braced myself for what I knew was coming. While waiting for the surgery date to arrive, I spent what felt like hundreds of hours doing Internet research on my particular form of cancer and the known surgical alternatives. I was determined to learn enough to be an active participant in the final choice of my treatment. I used my network of family and friends to find cancer and hysterectomy survivors I could talk to. The most creative suggestion I unearthed through these conversations was the notion of scheduling liposuction for the same day as my hysterectomy; in essence, getting two surgeries for the price of one and a half. The bargain shopper side of me was quite drawn to the idea. My more logical self questioned whether this was a good time to go bargain shopping.

Four days from D-Day, two of my male friends dragged me to the Sierras for a day of skiing. They didn't know how else to help. In honor of the occasion, I tried out a rental pair of high-end skis, and enjoyed them so much I purchased them at the end of the day. Owning a hot pair of skis seemed like a great way to guarantee I would regain my health. As it turned out, I did just that.

The morning of surgery, I was so nervous that I begged the anesthesiologist to put me out before I got anywhere near the operating room. He complied. By the time the anesthesia wore off, I was settled into the hospital room where I began my recovery and stayed for two nights. It only hurt when I moved. Unfortunately, breathing fell into that category.

Over time I healed, and resumed my life. The cancer, ultimately diagnosed as a slow-growing cancer that was found only in the location where the uterus meets the cervix, is now gone from my body. There were clean margins surrounding the cancerous tissue the doctor removed. This negated the need for radiation, chemotherapy, and other further treatment. Unfortunately, the doctor's recommendation included the words "there are no guarantees."

I know there are no guarantees, but I now find great joy in the simple act of writing items on the calendar for future months. And as a result of my season in hell, I have a newfound appreciation for the thin line between health and disease, and the permeable border between them. Now that I am "cancer-free" for many years, living life fully, however trite that sounds, is my sweet revenge. Just don't ask me to do another marathon. I'm feeling too good to risk it.

ON THE COUNT OF THREE

Susan Antolin

"ON THE COUNT OF THREE we're going under. One, two, three. . ."
My four-year-old comes up gagging and coughing. She has a
look of desperation on her small wet face, her hair plastered
across her cheeks, as she clings to the swim instructor's arms. Her
eyes dart over to where I sit, fully clothed and dry on the warm
cement, a towel printed with pink princess crowns in my arms. I
can taste the chlorine she swallows as I stifle the urge to end the
lesson early. The instructor speaks to her in a low voice, and my
daughter moves her head in an almost imperceptible nod up and
down. I watch as she goes under again, this time blowing bubbles
and emerging without a cough.

A few hours earlier I drove my mother to a doctor's appointment in San Francisco. Now, sitting on the pool deck, I wonder
if the doctor said, "On the count of three we're going under,"
when she told my mom the disease she has been running from for
years is back and attacking her skin. My mom emerged from the
examination room today with a look of drowning. Her hands
were shaking, and she took shallow breaths, as if there were not
enough air in the waiting room. She pulled a scrap of paper from
her purse and wrote the diagnosis. She clung to the paper,
although it could not hold her above water.

As we made our way back to the car, she looked at me with
the look of a small child waiting to be told what to do next. She
wanted to climb out of the pool. I told her we'll take it one step
at a time. We'll find a specialist. I had no dry towel to offer.

I used to think mothers had answers. Now that I am a mother
I know there are times we just make it up as we go along. On a
good day, I offer a dry towel. On other days, all I can do is bear
witness to the struggles around me.

My daughter goes under one last time and comes up gagging
again. This time she throws up on the instructor's shoulder. They
both climb out of the pool and head for the shower. The lesson is

over. We walk back home, my daughter wrapped in the princess towel, her hair dripping onto the sidewalk, the marks of goggles around her eyes, the battle over—for today.

LOSING IT

Marcie Beyatte

WHEN I WAS VERY YOUNG, I used to go to the beauty parlor with my grandmother and watch while she had her hair marcelled into soft waves. I'd collect abandoned scraps of hair on the floor and sort them into piles by color and then by shade. My own hair didn't belong to me yet: my mother was in charge and she would roughly wash, comb, and try to tame my curls with barrettes. It was always painful work.

A few years later, I had an exotic babysitter from Quebec named Justlynn who could be persuaded to do my hair in a French twist. We had to pilfer my mother's hair spray and hunt down every bobby pin in the house to get my mop to conform. After Justlynn was finished, I would sleep sitting up, so I could have one more day of beautiful hair.

When I was around eight, I'd sneak into my mother's bathroom and use her tube of Alberto VO5 Hairdressing Cream in an attempt to tame my hair. When I was caught, I was punished by being forbidden to go to Randi Nisker's birthday party. I was further humiliated because I had to tell Randi why.

As a teenager, my best friend and I scorched each other's hair as we ironed it between towels. My sisters swore that wrapping their hair around empty orange juice cans at night would make it go straight, but nothing worked for me. The time came to accept my curly-headed reality.

But two years ago, I took a chance and had my hair professionally straightened at a fashionable downtown salon. For the first time in my life, I loved my hair! It was shiny and smooth and I could toss it. For two weeks, I enjoyed blowing it dry and using new hair products.

Then a routine mammogram diagnosed breast cancer, and I learned I'd have to go through chemo and lose my hair. That I would also lose a breast seemed less traumatic at the time. For the six weeks before chemo started, I had a love affair with my hair, made sweeter knowing that we were soon to part.

Bridget, my chemo nurse, told me that in 18 to 22 days after my first treatment, my hair would start falling out. I asked if there were exceptions, and she firmly told me, "No." I didn't want to lose my hair, handful by handful, nor shave my head alone in a shameful room, so I invited my friends to witness the event. I wanted to be with people I loved and insisted they wear wigs or hats for the occasion. I bought a wig that was close in style to my straight hair to wear after the deed was done. The day of the party approached, and my hair was still stuck to my head. I checked it a few times a day. I feared that my hair wouldn't have started falling out by the party and my friends would be disappointed. Did I have the courage to shave my head before it started leaving on its own accord? What if I was the exception and Bridget was wrong?

At spin class three days before the party, I wiped sweat from the back of my neck and a big wad of hair stuck to my palm. I was relieved; the party could go on as planned.

From then on, I brushed my hair outside on my front lawn and took showers at the gym.

On the afternoon of my head-shaving party, my sister braided my hair into ten braids so I could donate it to Locks for Love, an organization that uses human hair to make wigs for kids undergoing chemo. My niece burned a CD of songs about hair, including David Crosby's lament, "Almost Cut My Hair," and the theme song from *Hair*.

My friends gathered in the garden wearing a hilarious assortment of wigs and hats. Even my dog, Chelsea, had a tiara. The wine flowed, and I almost forgot the purpose of the party.

My son began by cutting off my braids, and then my husband took over with the buzzer. The scissors hurt because the blades were dull and the sound of the buzzer was deafening, but soon, all that remained of my hair was a heap on the deck, already dispersing in the breeze. That I didn't harbor any disfiguring scars or carbuncles on my scalp was a relief, and my friends commented on my beautifully shaped head. I took a quick shower and made an entrance in my wig and a long caftan, like an old-fashioned starlet.

I dutifully wore my wig when I greeted the mailman and wore a kerchief at the gym. After two weeks of being compliant, I realized I was hiding my baldness as if I were ashamed. In spin class, beside my bald friend Zane, I ripped off my babushka, thinking that if he could be bald, so could I. I no longer felt like a badly made-up drag queen.

The hardest test was going grocery shopping bald. The first time I made the attempt, I had my wig beside me in the car. I cried as I chickened out and donned it at the last minute. The next time I succeeded, but I was convinced everyone was staring at me. After 10 or 20 times I forgot to notice, and after 50 or 60 times I forgot to care.

After my chemo treatments ended I went to the barbershop and asked Elroy, the barber, to get rid of the fuzz that remained. I wanted my new hair to come in "virgin," not tainted by chemo drugs. Elroy used warm shaving cream and a straight-edge razor to make my pate smooth and put hot towels on my head. It was the best haircut I'd ever had; I got exactly what I asked for. Elroy refused to accept payment, and my husband is now his faithful customer.

As my hair started growing, I examined it daily, but I was still bald for months. After three months, my hair looked like the gray lamb coat my Russian grandmother used to wear. After six months, I had steel-gray curls that lay close to my skull. After one year, I had a serious Afro in which I could hide small objects. I now used products for "women of color." After 18 months, close friends told me that I might consider wearing a hat. All the time.

It was time to make a decision; either I'd cut my hair into a more human shape or get it straightened. I chose to straighten it, and regained a smooth cap of hair covering my ears. My hair could once again blow in the wind. I felt like me again, as I tossed my hair.

At the Grammys this year, when Melissa Etheridge sang "Piece of My Heart" in memory of Janis Joplin, I felt as if it were only the two of us in the room. There she was, beautiful in her baldness, proud and strong, just like me.

A GIFT UNBIDDEN

Maureen Martin Appel

ON A GRAY, RAINY DAY just a few weeks before Thanksgiving I was in my car when news of Iris Chang's suicide spilled out of the radio. I had followed Iris's writing career and her research into World War II atrocities in China. Her international bestseller, *The Rape of Nanking*, had vaulted her to icon status in the Chinese-American community. The horror she had uncovered had been profound, and I'd read that Iris had been deeply affected; but still, I couldn't believe what I heard. The sidewalks were crowded with students and shoppers, and I wondered if anyone else felt the shock of her death.

Just days earlier, in a quiet candlelit ritual, I had marked the suicide anniversary of my mother, who was 36 when she over-dosed on 70 tablets of Phenobarbital. Iris, too, was 36 at the time of her death. But unlike my mother, she was a brilliant author and journalist—successful, ambitious, and admired, all qualities which I had assumed granted immunity from self-destruction. What ever prompted her to kill herself?

I lurched along College Avenue, listening in a daze to the terrible details—a gunshot wound to the head, her car discovered by a commuter. But the report of Iris leaving a two-year-old, her lone child, stopped me cold. I pulled over to the curb and killed the engine. *She was a mother?! How could she do it? How could she leave her baby? Why? What had happened?* The familiar lament had begun, and I had no way to silence it.

This is the peculiar terrain of children of suicide. No matter how much time goes by, the unanswerable questions persist: *Why did you leave me? How could you abandon young children? What brought you to such despair? Why couldn't you get help? What if I had washed the dishes, cleaned my room, mowed the lawn, painted the sky, sung an aria, tried harder to be perfect?* The engine of self-doubt thrums along, and the sense of abandonment and rejection never fully dissipates. Somewhere inside, the child lives, captured in a quiet, surreal diorama at the exact moment of loss.

Eventually I started the car and headed home. For days I felt depressed, confounded over Iris Chang's decision to end her life, and feeling a sense of loss for little baby Chang. I knew what the future held for him, a motherless journey, or at least a life without his birth mother. In my case, my mother's absence had thrust me into a state of recurring diffidence. No matter who steps in to fill the mother-void for a child of suicide, no matter how many other mothers, teachers, grandmothers, and aunts are borrowed, the question of self-worth arises. *If I had been more lovable (undamaged), she would not have left me.*

Suicide is the ultimate rejection of life, of self, of those left behind. There is no going back, no second chance, no talking through the searing emotional pain. It's just over. And all of the questions, the things unsaid, the missed opportunities, they're gone.

More than 40 years later, I still wonder how my life might have been different if my mother had lived. I'd like to think I would have grown up feeling less acutely sensitive to everyone else's needs, and more aware of my own requirements. And maybe I would have found my voice earlier, and my place in the world. When I listen to other women complain about their mothers for being overly intrusive or hypercritical or too passive, I wonder if my mother and I would have found common ground.

She died when I was 11, and from those early years of child-hood I remember very little. She was petite, just like my grand-mother and my sister, and she had the face of an angel—blue eyes, golden hair, the sweetest smile. When I was in kindergarten, she sewed a ballerina costume for me with pink sequins, black velvet, and stiff tulle netting. We once baked a cake in the shape of a star for my father. Her closet was lined with dozens of size two dresses and stacks of high heels, and she loved to dance to big-band tunes. But everything changed when she and my father divorced.

We moved south, and continued to move, five times in three years—from my grandmother's house to a small duplex, to a second-floor apartment, then the little house on St. Joseph Street, and finally to a bungalow one block from the ocean. My mother started to date younger men, and bought a convertible on credit. On at least one occasion she rode around our small beach town in a white bathing suit and enormous turquoise sunhat. It hurts me to write that, but it's true.

"Do you love me, Maureen?" she would ask randomly, and I would stand before her knowing even as I answered that my words were not enough. During one week of miserable loneliness while my siblings and I vacationed with our father, she dyed her hair red, then chestnut brown, then back to blond. Many signs of growing instability and deepening depression were manifest. I wonder now, how were they missed?

Recently I read a series of articles debating the merits of a suicide barrier on the Golden Gate Bridge. The faces of the jumpers were young and ordinary; some were smiling. It seemed a nonissue: if just one life could be saved with a barrier, wouldn't that be reason enough? I recalled a day months earlier when I had walked across the bridge into Sausalito with a friend. We were talking and laughing, reveling in the wild weather and the intense beauty all around us. But somewhere around the halfway mark I needed to hurry off, get away from the rail and the sickening physical terror in my body. I could not stop thinking of all the jumpers and the eerie, magnetic pull of the water below, a vast, beckoning womb which had lured so many people over. It was a frightening moment, not because of any fear for my life, but for the clear understanding of the simple ease with which life could end.

So many suicides are deemed a cry for help, an impulsive gesture intended more to relieve unyielding, crushing psychological pain rather than to end life. In my mother's case, I want to think that she was ambivalent in her last act, needing to escape, but only for a while. Perhaps today's antidepressants and/or psychotherapy might have alleviated her despair. She blamed herself for the breakup of the family, and she had no tools to mend the impossible shreds that her life had become. She had no one to go to for help. But who knows? Many of the bridge-jumpers were on medication or in therapy. Iris had been despondent and was seeing a psychiatrist, but by some accounts was not taking her prescribed meds at the time of her death.

My mother's sudden leave-taking left me and my siblings half-alive, traumatized, spinning in grief and darkness. My sister and brothers and I stood in profound need, and the adults were ripped apart by guilt. It was impossible not to second-guess everything, and think of all the ways she might have been saved. *If only, if only, if only. . .*

With the self-preservation of an 11-year-old, I returned to the sixth grade and stumbled through that bleak year. I wanted to protect my mother's memory, to become her, preserve her. I tried to wear her clothes, which were too small for me even then. Who was I, I wondered, apart from my mother?

Later as a young mother fueled by a new rage over my mother's abandonment of her children, I veered as far away as possible from her image. I wore Birkenstocks and braids, corduroy and denim, and refused to diet away the pounds gained from pregnancy, wanting to be everything my mother was not. But her perceived opposite was not the real me either.

As my children reached puberty, the uncharted path before me grew ever more perplexing. I wanted to give them everything that had been denied me: security, safety, warmth, order, sweetness. And yet it was I, the child caught inside, who most needed that nourishing environment. In a brief dream, my mother came to me dressed in a red woolen coat and scarf. We stood together on a platform high in the Alps against a backdrop of milky snow, waiting for the train to Zurich. I was a child of eight or nine, and as she held my hand I asked her, "Where are you taking me?"

That dream helped me go forward, initiating the pivotal work of my adult life. In the deepest of ironies, I know that the act of my mother's suicide was the catalyst for my beginning steps toward wholeness, a lifelong labor. Her suicide set in motion a motherless journey that propelled me to drop down into my own being and face the terror of my unworthiness. As it happened, her death precipitated a move to a different city, different schools, and a different intellectual environment which actively supported psychoanalysis. Would I have searched so purposefully for a deeper understanding of my life if my mother had lived? I cannot say. But had I not honored the dream imagery and allowed a different sort of journey to unfold, I imagine I would have remained a stranger to myself, bound in survival strategies and defense mechanisms, and unable to access my truest self.

For years I wrestled with my fate, unsure if I could be stitched together. I was afraid to trust, or to love without reservation, or claim happiness as my own. And yet many, many years later, here I am, loving deeply and deeply loved, liking who I am for the most part, valuing myself as a woman, as a mother, as a friend. Was my mother's last act a horrible gift, a terrible grace in a fearful disguise?

The little Chang baby probably won't remember much about his mother when he grows up, except what he will read about her in books and what his father will tell him. But when he learns that she took her own life, it will be difficult not to ask why. It will be difficult not to ask what if. It will be difficult to see a hidden gift.

DOG WALKS

Dorothy Moore

I'VE BEEN DREAMING about our dog. There was a point in my life when I had predictable dreams about sex. But I am almost 50, and last night I dreamed I was riding a broken bicycle with Daisy, our new Golden Retriever, seated on the handlebars. She looked at me with the familiarity of a lost friend and said we really needed to go for a walk. I told her what a good dog she is.

I let Daisy out at five this morning. Usually she comes bounding in with a stick to gnaw. This morning Daisy stayed outside, tugging on one of the volunteer willow trees my 19-year-old son recently felled. Instead of sawing the willows into smaller logs, as instructed, Duncan left two 20-foot poles, stripped of their branches, leaning against the playhouse. The beginnings of a backyard teepee, he explained. My back was too sore to take any counteraction. But Daisy had her own ideas. She had found a very big stick.

I called Daisy in, praised her, then proceeded to make coffee. But the big sticks made her anxious. She paced the kitchen, heading outside to gnaw, chew, and pull, then galloping back inside for praise. I explained that not all sticks can be retrieved. She is six months old. How can she know these things yet?

Daisy is snow-white with touches of champagne beige on her topcoat. She is an elegant dog, with feathers of fur around her neck, who looks deeply into my eyes with the sage expression of another dog I once knew and has the stealthy ability to find and gum stray socks as if they were hapless woodland creatures. Daisy is the successor to Copper.

Copper was a magnificent red Golden Retriever. He adopted us by following Duncan home from school when Duncan was in fourth grade. Though I was not the dog type, I could see that the kids were taken. So when I tracked down Copper's owner and found he was newly divorced, I hinted that the dog was always welcome at our house. Within a week we were dog owners.

Jim and his teenage daughter came over that Saturday with Copper, his dish, and his rabies certificate. Copper was already eight years old. Jim kept wiping back tears. His daughter hugged Copper. I said visit whenever you want. Don't be a stranger. They never did visit, but every now and then I see Jim around town. I haven't had the chance to tell him Copper passed away last spring at the ancient age of 17.

In fact, Copper lived two lives. At age ten he collapsed while I was walking him. Somehow I carried him half a mile home, pushed him into the car, and soon after, reluctantly agreed to dog surgery. The repair of his ruptured spleen did not go well. After three nights in dog critical care at $300 a night, excluding dog transfusions, I felt that we'd spent more money than prudent, and that since I am a nurse, I could keep a decent eye on the dog at home.

I brought Copper home after convincing our very kind vet to give me pain injections and several bags of IV fluid, which I hung from a ladder in the middle of the family room. I didn't expect Copper to last the night, but he did, wrapped in an electric blanket with me sitting next to him. For days the kids and I took turns squeezing chicken broth into his mouth, and then, as Copper healed, we spoon-fed him sautéed chicken breast.

During Copper's convalescence, something subtle transpired, and I became a dog person. I noticed the similarity between Copper and my husband—quiet, gentle, loyal. Instead of being insulted by the comparison, I believe Jeff was flattered. Once Copper was up and about, Jeff and I were more excited than Copper to go out for walks. "Look, Mom, it's Copper," said a neighbor girl when we walked him, his stomach still shaved bare from the surgery. Her Brownie troop had just toured the vet's and heard of Copper's amazing recovery. Copper was famous!

But Copper was a different dog: slower, yet wiser, more intuitive. Copper took Jeff on as his project. Jeff says he's not a workaholic, but evidence suggests to the contrary. If he is home, he is at his desk writing computer code. If he is not home, he is at work. His high-school yearbook foretells it all: "To the human computer," wrote one classmate. Copper decided it was his job to guard Jeff through his labors, to get him out for a little fresh air now and then.

For years Copper slept at Jeff's side whenever Jeff sat down to work. In turn, Jeff became the most reliable dog walker in the family. Rain or shine, Jeff made sure Copper got his daily walk. While it is difficult to convince Jeff to exercise, he felt it was his duty to walk Copper. And we always thought it was a lovely coincidence that Jeff and Copper shared the same June 1st birthday.

As Copper aged, his muzzle grew snow-white. His eyes clouded with cataracts. He became very stiff. Jeff shortened the walks, but tried to take two a day. Jeff, in his red windbreaker, and Copper, tottering alongside him, were a neighborhood item, moving at a snail's pace as if they had all day. I was too restless to join in, preferring to spend my outdoor time jogging or swimming.

Even if you are a shy person, you make friends when you walk a dog. While the dogs are smelling each other, tails wagging, their owners exchange greetings. If Jeff wasn't going to be home, he bugged me to walk Copper. When I took Copper out, one of our many dog friends would ask, "Isn't that your husband who walks that elderly dog? He's so patient."

When Copper could no longer stand up on his own and was incontinent both ways, my mornings started with a cleanup job, and then I set Copper outside to stumble about the backyard. It was getting weird, and the winter seemed endlessly wet and cold. I had to think, despite the brave effort, that Copper was in pain. But separating Jeff and Copper in a manner that was gentle, that was going to be a tricky business. Finally, after much soul-searching, I asked the vet if he would come out to the house. I talked to the family about the humane treatment of animals.

A date was set in April. But when I woke up that morning it was warm and sunny and Copper stood up on his own, something we hadn't seen for months. I canceled the appointment. A few days later, though, I called the vet again. It seemed as if it was time. When Jeff came home that night, even though I had warned him, he sat down at his desk and asked, "Where's Copper?" I wasn't sure if he was confused or attempting a bad joke, so I headed to the gym for a late-night swim with a lump in my throat.

As the weeks passed we didn't talk much about Copper's death, but occasionally would remember him fondly, especially when we saw one of our dog friends out for a walk. I think we all agreed that he was now in a more peaceful, pain-free place. Some people say it's better to wait awhile before you get another dog, but just four months after Copper left us, I heard of a litter up in Red Bluff. The puppy pictures were very cute and the breeder well recommended. Driving up the interstate, snow-capped Mt. Shasta loomed ahead, and we decided to name this dog Shasta Daisy.

Daisy sleeps by the window in Copper's old spot, guarding Jeff who walks her morning and night. She is learning about fetching, taking walks, and making friends. On my desk I keep a Christmas photo with the kids in their jammies, their hair wet from bath-time. They are hugging Copper, asleep with a smile on his wise face, tired after a long walk in the woods.

THE PARTY

Diana Divecha

MY HUSBAND Arjun turned 50 this year, and, prodded by his mother, I began to think about throwing a party for him. "Can adults have big birthday parties?" I wondered, as I speculated whether we could even gather enough people to make a party— he is from India and the spheres of his life spanned the globe. With modest expectations, we sent out 100 invitations. To our shock, 200 friends and family from all over the world RSVP'd: boarding-school and college buddies from India, colleagues and friends from London to Russia to Singapore, local friends and family. I plunged into a sea of doubt at the same time as I began to plan the dinner, entertainment, and dancing. Are we worthy of so much attention? Is it presumptuous to throw a big bash for one person? Will I be able to create an event that is good enough? Isn't there a more important, serious use of my time than arranging a party?

Midway into the details, all planning ground to a halt. My friend's 19-year-old son Max died accidentally from a drug over-dose, the end of a self-destructive spiral he'd struggled with for years. I cooked for my friend, talked with her, and vicariously plummeted myself. I thought of my friend and her son constantly. I'd seen over the years how hard she and her husband tried to save him, with state-of-the-art treatments, schools, counseling, love and support, but his biochemistry seemed to keep outrunning them all as he chose to opt out and self-medicate. He was a gifted songwriter, but even his devotion to music couldn't save him. He was close to my kids in age, and the echo rattled deeply. How does a mother surrender to sleep at night if her child has left the planet? In the morning, when I got up and looked in the mirror, my chest constricted with the thought of brushing my teeth if I'd lost a child. I began to hug my two daughters as if they'd returned from the dead.

For Max's memorial service, I helped out with the food. "Plan for 30 or so, 50 at the most," my friend directed me. To our aston-ishment, 200 people packed and overflowed the tiny memorial chapel. For two hours, old people stood silently next to weeping teenagers, no one even shifting feet, as they were riveted in somber engagement with the family. Max's spirit soared into the chapel when his own music started to play. The lyrics were blunt and raw, and his sweet boyish tenor contrasted with the heavy metal guitar distortions in the background. He seemed to be singing to us from afar, from somewhere at the height of the chapel ceiling, telling his story, pleading for relief. Friend after friend came forward to attest to Max's presence in their lives, and we heard how he was so much more than his struggles—we learned that he would blurt out the truth in delicate circumstances, that he made deep friends with homeless people, that he was intensely sensitive. "I loved Max, we shared everything," said a teen friend. "Even though we drifted apart, he was such an important part of my childhood," said another. "If Max knew how many people cared about him, cared that he existed, maybe he would have tried harder to stay here," his mom said to me afterwards.

A few days later, I dragged myself back to planning a party. Sobered by Max's death and sympathetic to my friend's feelings, I felt frivolous to be combing through old photographs, planning a program. Life can turn suddenly, and in a phone call, an e-mail, a choice, an act, one can lose a loved one, and here I was planning jokes about my husband's girth, his vices, his ego. Yet something began to take shape as I made choices about how to craft the presentation of Arjun's life to display to others at his birthday party. As I knit together a PowerPoint story of his Indian child-hood, his own father's death, his immigration to America, his successful business and loving family, I realized that I was doing for him what Max's family had done for him. Except Arjun got to hear his story. From housekeeper and hairdresser, to auntie who changed his nappies, to family, to financial power brokers, people paused for the evening to wish him well in so many ways. We heard about how he goofs off at work, how he still carries his childhood pillow, and how he is a man of no small ego. And too, we heard how he mattered: That his college roommate has never found a more loving friend, that he mentored one employee, inspired another. By the time Arjun himself finally got up to speak, the effects of these words were clear. Though uncharacteristically speechless, he was full up, sated, his chest nearly bursting with the love and goodwill of the many people that anchor his life.

The surprising turnout both for Max's funeral and for Arjun's birthday spoke to the desire, perhaps even the need, of others to bear witness to a loved one's life if given the opportunity. It is part of the human social contract. As Max let go and moved on, his music seemed to bind us to that karmic promise. Though the addictive process that Max struggled with was powerful, the voltage of an entire community's expression in unison was also powerful. As I planned Arjun's party, I remembered my friend's words. Was Arjun worthy of the time and expense of 200 people? Everybody is. Because hearing how you matter in this world might just make the difference someday between staying tethered to this life and letting go.

CONTRIBUTORS

Born in Italy, RINA ALCALAY grew up in Argentina and Chile. At 26 she came to the United States and earned her M.A. in Education and Ph.D. in Communication at Stanford. She has been a professor at UCLA and UC Davis, specializing in cross-cultural health communication and publishing widely in this area. Rina lives in Berkeley with her husband; they have a son, 26, and a daughter, 19.

SUSAN ANTOLIN's poetry appears regularly in poetry journals and has won several awards. She is a non-practicing attorney and mother of three young children living in Walnut Creek, California, where she writes in between swim meets and soccer games, at red lights, and in the occasional quiet of her kitchen. She is working on an individual collection of short poems.

MAUREEN MARTIN APPEL is a fourth-generation Californian who lives in Oakland amid the ghosts of her Irish ancestors. She has written for *Nine Lives*, the oral history project of the San Francisco–based Eldergivers, and also for the food section of the *Contra Costa Times*. A longtime docent at the UC Botanical Garden, she is currently teaching her new grandson the names of her favorite trees.

MARCIE BEYATTE is a breast cancer survivor/activist and the founder of "Cancer in So Many Words," a program created to encourage cancer survivors to write about their experiences. She is currently working on a number of fiction projects.

RONNIE CAPLANE is an attorney, Piedmont School Board member, and commissioner on the Compensation Appeals Board. From '97 to '03 she wrote the column "Under Construction" for Oakland's *Montclarion*. She has two children.

SWATHI DESAI was born in India and raised in the United States. She is a graduate of the University of Pennsylvania's Wharton School. After a 12-year career as a women's accessories designer, she is now a full-time mother. She dreams about the day when she will have time to compose more than the grocery list.

DIANA DIVECHA savors cross-cultural family life in Berkeley with her Indian-born husband and two teenage daughters. A developmental psychologist, she finds that her favorite topics to write about are, naturally, children, families, and the process of change and growth. Thanks to Wednesday Writers, she is a frequent contributor to *The East Bay Monthly*.

Using personal experience as her subject, KATHLEEN FARADAY co-wrote the column, "DoubleTalk," for ten years for the *Contra Costa Sun*. She has lived in the Philippines, Australia, Korea, and Hong Kong and all across the U.S. from Winnemucca, Nevada and Boise, Idaho to New York and Alabama. Piano and golf lessons, hiking, biking, skiing, and cooking are squeezed in between her job with BioView, USA, a molecular diagnostic company, and time with her six grandchildren.

ELIZABETH FISHEL has led the Wednesday Writers workshop for 15 years and added a Friday Writers group four years ago. She has also taught at the UC Berkeley Graduate School of Journalism and for many years at the University of California/Berkeley Extension. The author of four books—*Sisters, The Men in Our Lives, I Swore I'd Never Do That*, and *Reunion*—she has written widely for magazines including *Vogue, Oprah's O, Redbook, Parents, Family Circle, The New York Times Book Review*, and has been a Contributing Editor at *Child*. She lives in Oakland with her husband, and they have two sons.

LEAH POTTS FISHER is a psychotherapist and consultant on work/family balance. Married with two grown children, she has long been fascinated, professionally and personally, with the challenges and complexities of relationships. Currently, she is on sabbatical, traveling the world on her own, with visits and warm support from her husband.

MARY FORD is a mother, professional vocalist, and psychologist. She lives in Berkeley with her husband Rob and son Dan. Her other interests besides writing include dancing, meditating, and telling shaggy dog jokes.

LINDA GOLDFARB is an accidental vintner with her husband Steve, a recovering attorney. They left the "simple" life in San Francisco to pursue the hectic life in Napa Valley, making Cabernet at their winery, Anomaly Vineyards, in St. Helena, California. Linda's stories have appeared in *The San Francisco Chronicle, El Cerrito Journal*, and *Pet Companion*, among others. Linda has three rescued dogs, three sons, one daughter, and two grandchildren.

JEANNE HALPERN is a writer, editor, college professor, communications consultant, wife, mother, widow, grandmother, domestic partner, friend. Her writing has appeared in *Parents'* magazine, *The New York Times*, *Woman's Day*, and many academic journals. Of her four books, her favorite is a biography of her husband, who died when her children were quite young, written for their high school graduations.

TRISH HAWTHORNE loves architecture, old houses, and researching local history as well as tracking down the perfect gingersnap. A graduate of UC Berkeley, she worked as a teacher before becoming an independent college adviser. As such, she helps students find the recipe for the right college match.

TERRI HINTE was born in New York and "actualized" in California, where she has studied and intermittently practiced astrology, feng shui, I Ching, Tarot, massage, Feldenkrais, yoga, Pilates, horseback riding, dog training, bike repair, photography, horticulture, Portuguese, Czech, French, Italian, German, gospel singing, classical piano, samba and salsa dancing, tango, and writing. By day, she is a music publicist.

On any sunny day, you can find MELANIE JOHNSTON roaming the East Bay hills with her Bernese Mountain Dog, Abby, and her Pug puppy, Floyde. The work that she writes on rainy days has appeared on television, radio, and in the *San Francisco Chronicle*. She recently completed a memoir about World War II called *What My Father Saw* and is currently working on a novel, *Canines for Christ*.

SUZANNE LA FETRA's writing has appeared in the *San Francisco Chronicle* magazine, *Working Mother*, several literary journals, and on KQED-FM. She lives in northern California with her family, and is at work on a memoir.

MARIAN MAGID was a consultant in public relations and strategic planning, a contributing writer for several Bay Area newspapers, and an avid community volunteer. She was also an award-winning Director of Communications for both the Oakland Unified School District and the Contra Costa County Office of Education, representing 18 school districts. Her greatest love was her family: her husband Albert, three children, and six grandchildren. Marian died of cancer in 2007 at 72.

KERRY MESSER is working on her first novel and, next to being a mother, finds writing to be the most rewarding and challenging adventure yet. Having begun as a one-year sabbatical from a career as an Executive Coach and Organizational Consultant, her writing has become a life-long journey of self-discovery and a perpetually renewing exercise in humility.

KRISTINE K. MIETZNER earned a B.A. from the University of Washington and an M.S. in Education from California State University East Bay. She worked as a broadcast journalist in Alaska, raised a son and daughter, and taught in California public schools. Kristine welcomes personal experience stories for the book she is writing on thriving after divorce. She can be reached at kristinekaymietzner@hotmail.com.

JANIS MITCHELL always meant to write someday and joining the Friday Writers has given voice to this intention. She has found great satisfaction from processing her life in the personal essay form. She is very grateful to be associated with Elizabeth and the dynamic women of this group. Janis lives in Berkeley with her husband John and daughter Molly.

DOROTHY MOORE lives with her husband, three children, and dog Daisy in Lafayette. She is an ICU nurse who swims whenever she can.

BEATRICE MOTAMEDI is a graduate of the Creative Writing program at Stanford University, and she has worked as a reporter, writer, and editor for various publications, including *WebMD*, *Hippocrates*, *Newsweek*, and the *San Francisco Chronicle*. Currently, she teaches English and journalism at Oakland Technical High School.

A transplanted New Englander enjoying life in the Bay Area, KAREN MULVANEY is in the latter rounds of motherhood and taking stock of the upcoming years. After her mother's death from cancer and her own cancer diagnosis, she found chronicling her experiences a way to relax, understand, and bring meaning to life's joys and sorrows. She cherishes time with her friends and her growing family, which now includes five grandchildren.

MARY-JO MURPHY is learning Spanish. She now knows that the translation of the name of the town where she lives means luck. Nearly four years ago she moved to Ventura from Oakland. Since then, her life has been a challenge and adventure. As a Diabetes Educator in a hospital for an underserved, mostly Hispanic population she listens, advises, teaches, and counsels. As a writer she observes.

CHRISTY MYERS is a painter who discovered she also loves to paint with words. During her travels in Italy, France, Mexico, and throughout the U.S., she has painted *en plein air* and kept journals of her trips. She is working on an illustrated account of such a trip to Paris, as well as a book based on her family history in and around San Francisco.

PHYLLIS NAGLE, active alumna of the University of California, Berkeley, is a lifetime Bay Area resident. After shelving her MBA, obtained for a former career in business, she sought out Wednesday Writers and is now writing full-time. Phyllis has contributed to *Knight Ridder* and *Adams Media* publications. Her favorite summer reunion is at Lair of the Bear with her all-Cal family and six young grandchildren.

ELLEN NEWMAN is a San Francisco–based freelance writer and public relations specialist for the San Francisco Design Center. She writes about interior design and her experiences during a six-month trip to Southeast Asia.

PATTY NORTHLICH was born in New York City. She received a B.A. in Political Science from Northwestern University. She lived in France and Switzerland before marrying a Marine Corps aviator and eventual computer scientist, whose career has kept them in the San Francisco Bay area for 35 years. Patty is the mother of a son and daughter, both performing artists, who live in New York City. Her passions are swimming and tap dancing.

Born in the Northeast with a longing for the West, TRENA NOVAL now lives in California. For the last ten years she was a contributing editor and writer for an arts journal, but lately she has been focusing her writing time on other pursuits, such as family and exploring life from behind the wheel of her car. She was recently part of the *Nine Lives, Vol. 2: Writing With Elders* life stories project for the Bay Area.

RISA NYE is Associate Director of College Counseling at Oakland's Head-Royce School and author of *Road Scholar, A Journal for the College Bound Student*. She is a volunteer tutor at 826 Valencia in Francisco, and her essays and articles have appeared in several publications. Risa lives with her husband in Oakland. Her father, Sam Elkind, always told her she should be a writer and would not be at all surprised.

CHRISTINE PARSONS weaves humor and heart into family-centered narratives. Her essays have been published in the *San Francisco Chronicle*, *East Bay Monthly*, *Oakland Tribune*, and *Orange County Register* and in the book *In Real Life: Powerful Lessons from Everyday Living*. She received an MFA from St. Mary's College of California and lives in Danville with her husband and children.

KAREN L. PLISKIN lives in Oakland with her husband and daughter. She has a Ph.D. in Anthropology and Middle Eastern Studies from Harvard University, and more than a decade's experience on the faculty of the University of California San Francisco. Karen left academia to pursue creative writing and art, and wishes government policy-makers would listen to her.

LORI ROSENTHAL is a marketing consultant, wife, mother of two teenage daughters, and consummate volunteer whose greatest writing pleasure is to capture the humor embedded in daily life. Lori especially appreciates the fact that the computer keyboard never talks back and doesn't need rides home from BART or soccer practice.

KATE RUDDLE is a writer, performer, and exhibiting artist in the Bay Area. She received her MFA in Sculpture from the San Francisco Art Institute and currently teaches drawing at Las Positas College in Livermore. Originally from Connecticut, she drove to California with her dog in 1992.

Born in New York to Greek parents, IRENE SARDANIS is a clinical psychologist in private practice. She lives with her husband in Oakland. Irene's first published piece appeared in 2003 in the *Psychotherapy Networker*.

LAURA SHUMAKER lives in Lafayette, California with her husband Peter and her three teenage boys. She recently completed a memoir about life with an autistic son, *A Regular Guy*, and is a regular contributor to NPR Perspectives. Her work has also been published in the *San Francisco Chronicle*, *The Autism Perspective*, the *Contra Costa Times*, and *Guideposts Magazine*.

MARTHA SLAVIN is continuing her cyclical life: artist, teacher, writer, wife, mother, community worker, traveler. After spending five years living in Japan and France meeting the challenges of new languages and cultures while maintaining a stable family environment, she and her family (husband Bill, 18-year-old son Theo) are back in the U.S.A. adjusting to the reverse cultural shock of coming home. These experiences are now the focus of her writing.

JOAN STEVENSON relishes the hours she can call her own since waving goodbye to the 9-to-5 grind and saying hello to Social Security. Her writing takes a reflective look at her roles as a daughter, wife, mother, and aging crone.

SARAH WEINBERG grew up in New York City. She received her B.A. in anthropology from Ohio Wesleyan University, and also holds a master's degree in clinical social work from Columbia University. She has a full-time private practice, and autobiographical writing is one of her sub-specialties. Her writing has appeared in *Becoming Whole: Writing Your Healing Stories*.

KAREN YENCICH is an advertising/marketing professional, freelance writer, and mother of two living in Berkeley.

CREDITS

Some of the poems in Sue Antolin's "Artichoke Season" have appeared in *Modern Haiku, American Tanka, Frogpond, Mariposa, Asahi Shimbun, Tanka Calendar 2005* (Winfred and Clinging Vine Press), *something like a sigh; Tanka Society of America 2005 Members' Anthology, Tanka Splendor 2005* (AHA Books).

Marcie Beyatte, "Losing It" appeared in *The Contra Costa Times*, April 16, 2005.

Ronnie Caplane, "The Shoe" appeared in *The Montclarion*, August 1, 2003.

Diana Divecha, "The Party" appeared in *The San Francisco Chronicle* magazine, November 12, 2006.

Diana Divecha, "The Puja" appeared in *The East Bay Monthly*, July 2005.

Diana Divecha, "Language of Silence" appeared in *The East Bay Monthly*, June 2004.

Kathleen Faraday, "A Normal Grandma" appeared in *The Contra Costa Sun*, March 12, 2003.

Kathleen Faraday and Joan Stevenson, "The Secret of Life is in the Silverware" appeared in *The Contra Costa Sun*, April 21, 2004.

Kathleen Faraday, "Stopped in My Tracks" appeared in *The Contra Costa Sun*, June 24, 2005.

Elizabeth Fishel, "How to Spice Up Your Life" appeared in *Oprah's O* magazine, January 2003.

Elizabeth Fishel, "Same Time Next Year" appeared in *Child* magazine, February 2003.

Terri Hinte, "Accordion Dreams" appeared in *Passionfruit* magazine, Winter 2000.

Suzanne LaFetra, "Still Life With Flowers" appeared in *Tattoo Highway*, January 2005.

Suzanne LaFetra, "Warm Enough" appeared in *The Christian Science Monitor*, January 12, 2006.

Marian Magid, "Romance in Winter" appeared in *The Contra Costa Times*, February 12, 2005.

Trena Noval, "Water Dreams" appeared on KQED's "Perspectives," February 10, 2006.

Risa Nye, "The Enchanted Castle Cake" appeared in *The San Francisco Chronicle* magazine, August 29, 2004.

Risa Nye, "Shaving" appeared in *The East Bay Monthly*, June 2005.

Christine Parsons, "Malt-o-Matic" appeared in *The East Bay Monthly*, June 2005.

Irene Sardanis, "The Tree" appeared in *Psychotherapy Networker*, November/December 2003.

Laura Shumaker, "A Regular Guy" appeared in *The San Francisco Chronicle* magazine, January 15, 2006.

Joan Stevenson, "Tiramisu or S'Mores" appeared in *The Contra Costa Times*, July 27, 2005.

Karen Yencich, "Singing with the Okay Chorale" appeared in *The Contra Costa Times*, March 27, 2004.